*To Peter, with love   A.S.*

Text copyright © 2011 Andrea Skevington
This edition copyright © 2016 Lion Hudson

Published by Lion Books
an imprint of
**Lion Hudson plc**
Wilkinson House, Jordan Hill Road,
Oxford OX2 8DR, England
www.lionhudson.com/lion

ISBN 978 0 7459 7664 8
e-ISBN 978 0 7459 7671 6

First edition 2016

**Acknowledgments**
The Bible retellings are based on the corresponding passages in the Holy Bible, New International Version and the Good News Bible.

The Holy Bible, New International Version Anglicised is copyright © 1979, 1984, 2011 Biblica, formerly International Bible Society. Used by permission of Hodder & Stoughton Ltd, an Hachette UK company. All rights reserved. "NIV" is a registered trademark of Biblica. UK trademark number 1448790.

The Good News Bible © 1994 is published by the Bible Societies/HarperCollins Publishers Ltd UK, Good News Bible© American Bible Society 1966, 1971, 1976, 1992. Used with permission.

The Lord's Prayer as it appears in Common Worship: Services and Prayers for the Church of England (Church House Publishing, 2000) is copyright © The English Language Liturgical Consultation and is reproduced by permission of the publisher.

A catalogue record for this book is available from the British Library

Printed and bound in Malaysia, December 2015, LH01

# THE BIBLE STORY

*retold in twelve chapters*

BY ANDREA SKEVINGTON

**LION**

# Contents

# STORIES OF THE BEGINNING

## *Beginning*

So this is how it all began: with God, who created the heavens and the earth. At first, all was empty and dark: there was no shape or form. And the Spirit of God was there, hovering over the black, boundless waters.

Then, into this darkness, God spoke: "Let there be light!" and it appeared – the first ever light – dazzling and shimmering, bright beyond words. God saw that it was good. Then God split light from dark, day from night. So evening passed and morning came: the first day.

God spoke again: "Let all the water and air that flows and moves be divided up. Separate the blue above from blue below." So the wide expanse of sky unfolded, shining and full of light. Then evening passed and morning came: the second day.

God spoke: "Let the waters under the sky be gathered, so land can appear." So it was. The waters flowed together, and glistening land began to emerge from the waves.

God spoke: "Let the land produce plants – an abundance of every kind: trees that bear fruit and plants that bear seeds." And so the land began to shimmer with soft new growth; the whole earth was greening, fresh and new – like the first ever spring day. God saw that it was good. So evening passed and morning came: the third day.

God spoke: "Let lights shine in the sky to mark day and night, the turning of the seasons, and the passing of the years." So there was the greater light, the sun, for the day, and the smaller, the moon, for the night. God also made the countless shining stars. And God saw that it was good. Then evening passed and morning came: the fourth day.

God spoke: "Let the waters be filled with life, shimmering with creatures, and let flights of birds soar through the sky." And so the seas heaved with living things: huge fish, tiny shells, silvery eels, and strange creatures of the deep; and the air was filled with the songs of birds flying high and free. God saw that it was good, and blessed all the creatures, telling them to live and grow and flourish. So evening passed and morning came: the fifth day.

God spoke: "Let the land produce all sorts of living creatures!" And so creatures began to appear on the land: the great and the small, the wild animals, and those that moved slowly across the ground. God saw that it was good. But there was more. God spoke again. "Let us make human beings to be like us, so they can be responsible for the fish of the sea and the birds of the air, and for the whole of the living earth." And so God created human beings: male and female. God blessed them and told them to grow in number. God gave them every plant that bore seeds, and the fruit of the trees, for their food.

God looked at all that he had made; everything was beautiful, vibrant, growing, and blessed. God saw that it was all very good. So evening passed and morning came: the sixth day.

Then, on the seventh day, God rested from his work of bringing life from darkness and nothingness. God blessed the day of rest for all creation, for all time.

# The garden

God formed Adam and Eve, the first man and the first woman, and breathed into them the breath of life. God made a paradise to be their home: the garden of Eden. God put them in the garden so they could work its rich soil, and care for it together. The garden was lush and green for it was watered by a great river, and at its heart were two trees: the Tree of Life and the Tree of the Knowledge of Good and Evil. Adam and Eve lived near their spreading shade. How happy and at peace they were, for everything was perfect and beautiful. They had no need of clothes, for they felt no shame.

God told them, "This is a place of plenty! The trees everywhere are heavy with fruit. But you cannot pick all of it. There is one tree whose fruit you must not eat: the Tree of the Knowledge of Good and Evil. If you eat its fruit, you will die!"

# The slippery serpent

The bright serpent, cunning and full of lies, slid quietly through the soft green leaves of the garden. When it came to the woman, it stopped. "Did God really say that you should not eat the fruit of any tree?" it hissed.

Eve replied, "We may eat the fruit of all these trees, but God did say that we should not eat from one tree in the middle of the garden. If we do, we will die!"

"No!" The serpent spoke softly, coiling itself around Eve. "You will not die. This is what will happen. You will see clearly what is good and what is evil, just as God does. You will become like God."

The serpent's twisted words set a trap for Eve, which tightened with every step she took toward the tree. Soon she could think of nothing else. How good the fruit looked! She had forgotten God's command, and she had forgotten the sweet fruit that hung from every other tree. She longed instead for the knowledge of good and evil, so she stretched out her hand and plucked the fruit, and shared it with Adam. As they bit into the fruit, they saw everything clearly.

They realized they were naked, so they hurried to gather fig leaves, stitching them together to make clothes to hide behind. Everything was changed.

Later Adam and Eve heard God walking in the garden in the cool of the evening, and they drew back into the shadows, hidden among the leaves. God called out, "Where are you?" and Adam stepped out of the darkness, his head bent low.

"I was afraid, because I was naked..." His voice shook as he spoke.

"Who told you that?" asked God. "Have you eaten the fruit I told you not to eat?"

So Adam and Eve told the whole broken-hearted tale of the snake's trap, and the shared fruit.

Then they trembled under God's curse. God spoke first to the snake, and then to Adam and Eve. "You, snake, will crawl in the dust all your days, the enemy of human beings. As for Adam and Eve: from now on, your lives will be hard, and scarred with pain. Even the land will sprout thorns instead of food because of what you have done. You will die, and return to the dust of the earth from which you were made."

God spoke again: "Adam and Eve must not be allowed to reach out and pick the fruit of the Tree of Life. If they eat it, their evil will live for ever. They cannot stay here in Eden, under the shade of the Tree of Life."

So God sent Adam and Eve out of the garden. They walked away weeping, their heads in their hands. As they looked back, they saw shining, wide-winged cherubim guarding the path back to the Tree of Life with a flashing, flaming sword.

They searched for somewhere else to make their home, but wherever they went, there was nowhere like Eden.

## Bloodstained ground

In time, Adam and Eve found a place to settle and had two sons. The elder, Cain, worked the land, and the younger, Abel, kept flocks of sheep. They had not forgotten God. When they came to make an offering to God, Cain quickly gathered up some of the crops he had grown, but Abel carefully chose the finest pieces of meat from the firstborn of his animals. God saw that Abel was offering the very best he could, and smiled on him. He was not so pleased with Cain's offering.

Cain strode around the fields with a face like thunder, knuckles clenched and white. God spoke to him: "Why are you so angry? Do what is right, and all will be well. Evil desires are lurking close by, waiting for you. Do not let them trap you. You can, you must, overcome them."

But Cain did not listen. He marched up to Abel. "Let's go into the fields," he said. Cain led his brother far away, where Adam and Eve could not hear them. Then he grabbed Abel and struck him again and again with all his angry, jealous strength. Abel's startled cries rang out in the silence as he fell to the ground. Then he lay still, broken and bleeding. There was no breath left in his body. Cain turned away, and walked back alone.

Then God said, "Cain, where is your brother Abel?"

"How should I know? It's not my job to keep track of him."

"Oh, Cain, what have you done? Don't you know that your dead brother's blood is crying out to me from the ground? Now that blood-soaked ground is cursed for you. It will no longer give you crops, and you will have to wander the face of the earth with nowhere to call home."

So Cain left, and Adam and Eve were alone. One son was dead, the other was his murderer. How empty the fields seemed.

## The waters break their bounds

Years passed, and many generations of people lived and died, until a time came when people had forgotten God. They did not resist evil but allowed it room in their hearts. They began to hate, and hurt, and cause each other misery and pain. God looked at what had become of the people he had made – made to be like him – and was filled with sorrow. "Enough!" he cried. "It's time to start again. Creation is ruined. I'll wash it all away."

But there was one person who did not join in with the evil-doers. His name was Noah, and he had not forgotten God. So God made him the centre of his plan to put everything right.

"You know how bad things are – the world is full of violence and hatred," God said to Noah. "This is what I'm going to do. I'm going to send rain and floods to destroy the earth. You must build a boat. Build it out of the finest timber, coated inside and out with tar so it will be watertight. It needs to be huge – wider and longer and taller than any boat you have ever seen. Gather your whole family together: your wife, your sons, and your daughters-in-law. Then bring animals into the ark – a male and female of every kind. You will also need food for them all.

"Now I make you a solemn promise – a covenant. I will keep you and your family, and all the creatures who sail in your ark, safe. So get to work!"

Noah did just as he was told. He built the huge ark on the dusty earth far from the sea. When he had finished, he stepped back. It towered above him. Then, as he was looking up, he saw the bright sky filling with thick, black, swirling clouds. Noah hurried to gather together a male and female of every creature in creation. He led the animals into the ark two by two, through grey, stinging rain. It fell day and night, night and day. The streams and springs became bubbling, muddy fountains pouring out water from the deep. The blue sky was blotted out.

The rains swamped valleys and plains, and crept up the sides of the mountains, until all was swallowed up in black, endless water. As they drifted helplessly over it, Noah and his family knew that all living things left behind on the land had been drowned. They were alone on the ark. When, after 40 days, the rain finally stopped, the silence was as cold as the waters.

Noah's family loved their precious cargo of animals: the only other living, breathing creatures left on the earth. They fed them, and cared for them. As they did so, a wind blew, and the waters began to sink slowly down. Then, one day, they heard the keel of the ark beneath them scraping and shuddering. The ark juddered to a halt, for it had struck the top of a mountain.

Every day they scanned the horizon, longing for land, and after many weeks they saw distant purple mountains breaking free of the water. Noah waited 40 more days, then set a raven free. It criss-crossed over the waves, looking for somewhere to perch. But there was nowhere.

A week later Noah tried again, sending out a dove. It came back with an olive twig. Noah held the bird tenderly in his hand, hope rising within him.

A week later he sent the dove out again. This time, it did not come back. It must have found somewhere to perch. At last, the flood was drying up! Noah's face broke into a wide smile as glistening land slowly emerged and dried.

Still they waited and waited. Then, at last, the flood had gone, and they opened the ark; and out tumbled the people and all the animals, the birds, and all manner of tiny creatures. Noah's family danced and laughed as the animals leaped and stretched, and the birds soared in the sky. How good it was to feel ground under their feet again! To have space to run and breathe freely! It was over, and time to give thanks. So Noah piled up rocks to form an altar and made an offering to God. Then the sun broke through the clouds and a perfect, shimmering rainbow appeared.

God said, "Remember this great promise, this covenant, I am making with the whole earth. Never again will the waters become a flood that destroys all life. When you see a rainbow, remember this promise!"

So the people smiled again, blessed by God, who told them there was to be no more killing. God said that they should live and grow and prosper. It was to be a new beginning under God's bright promise.

# The Family of Israel

## *The land, the promise, and Abraham*

Abraham took one last look behind him at the great city of Ur, with its narrow, crowded streets, and cool buildings made of hard-baked mud. It was his birthplace, but it would no longer be his home. His father was leaving for the distant land of Canaan, and Abraham was going with him. So they set off, with Abraham's wife Sarah, who was childless, and his nephew Lot, who was an orphan. When they had travelled as far as Haran they stopped and settled, their dreams of reaching Canaan fading with the passing years.

"Get up! It's time to go!" God said to Abraham. "You must leave your father's household and go to the land I will show you, the land of Canaan. I want to bless you and make your family into a great people. Through you, my blessing will flow to everyone on the earth."

So Abraham set off for this unknown land, with his wife Sarah and nephew Lot, and all their possessions, animals, and servants. Their long convoy travelled slowly. Sometimes they followed great river valleys, where the grass grew green. Other times they travelled across wide plains, throwing up clouds of dust from the hot earth. They journeyed through many lands on their way to Canaan, and drew more people to them as they went. When they camped at night, it looked like a town of tents, and by day their flocks stripped the land of green plants. Lot's shepherds and Abraham's shepherds began to grumble at each other. Soon, scuffles were breaking out over the best grazing.

"Let's not quarrel!" Abraham said to Lot. "This is a good land, and we are as close as brothers. Why don't we give each other some room? If you go one way, I'll go the other!"

Lot looked out at the land stretching away to the east. "It looks like God's garden of Eden, or the banks of the River Nile in Egypt!" he said. So Lot settled in the plain of the River Jordan, pitching his tents near the cities of Sodom and Gomorrah. And as he left, God reminded Abraham of his promise. "Just look around you – look at the good land stretching out before you. I will give it to you and your children. I will make your descendants like the grains of dust on the earth – uncountable. Now go and walk through the whole length and breadth of this land, your new home."

Abraham packed up his camp and walked through the land, pitching his tents again at a place known as Hebron, under the cool shade of its great trees. It was a good place, but Abraham was dwelling on God's promise. God had said he would give the land to Abraham and his children. But he and Sarah had no children, and they were now old.

Abraham and Sarah lived in the land God gave them, respected by those around them. All who lived in Canaan could see how God blessed them, and that Abraham was a good, wise man. But still the years passed and no child came.

"Do not be afraid!" God said. "Look up at the stars in the heavens. Your children will be like that!" And in time, Abraham came to believe God's promise.

Sarah longed for a child, but knew that her time for childbearing had passed. In her sadness she gave her maid, Hagar, to Abraham.

And Hagar had a son, Ishmael. Now, Hagar looked down on her childless mistress, and Sarah was sadder than ever.

## The three visitors

One day, Abraham was sitting by the entrance to his tent, sheltering from the fierce sun, when he saw three strangers standing a little way off. They shimmered in the heat. He ran up to them, and bowed low.

"Please, come and rest a while. Let me fetch food and water. It's too hot to travel with nothing in your stomachs!" And so they came.

Meanwhile, Abraham hurried to tell Sarah, "Get fine flour, and bake them some bread." Then he found a good calf in his herd and told his servant to prepare it for them. While they ate, Abraham stood near by, listening to their message.

"We'll be back this time next year. By then God will have blessed Sarah with a son!" Sarah could hear this from behind the tent, and began to laugh to herself. "Nothing is impossible for God!" said the messengers. "Sarah will have a son, whether she laughs or not!"

Sarah was frightened. "I didn't laugh!"

"Oh yes, you did!" they said.

## Saving Lot

The three strangers got up to leave, and Abraham kept them company for a while. They went down toward Sodom, where Lot lived.

God spoke to Abraham. "The people of Sodom and Gomorrah are full of evil. I've heard the cries of their victims. It's got to stop!

I will destroy the towns." Abraham gasped, and began to plead for Lot and his family.

"Will you sweep away the good with the bad? What if there are ten good people in the city – would you spare it?"

God listened to Abraham. "Yes, I would spare it if there were ten good people there."

Lot, meanwhile, was by the city gates. He saw the strangers approaching, and welcomed them. "Come and rest in my house. It's getting late." So they went to Lot's house.

But an ugly crowd gathered outside, threatening the strangers. "You must leave this place, for it will be destroyed," the strangers warned Lot. As dawn broke the next day, the strangers hurried him, his wife, and daughters out of the city. "Go now, don't look back and don't stop running or you will be swept away!" Then Lot and his family ran for their lives, hiding in the town of Zoar, while fire tore across the plain, swallowing up Sodom and Gomorrah. But Lot's wife turned back and watched the fire and the sulphurous rain, and was overcome. She never moved again.

The next morning, Abraham looked down at the smoking ruins. God had protected Abraham's family, the only ones who were not caught up in the city's evil.

## Joy and weeping

God had promised Sarah a child, and he was as good as his word. "When our son was born, God gave me joy and laughter," she said, so Abraham called his son Isaac, which means "he laughs". But even as Isaac grew, jealousy still gnawed at Sarah's heart.

"Get rid of that slave woman Hagar and her son!" she said to Abraham – but Abraham loved Ishmael, his firstborn. What would become of his first family if he sent them away? Abraham's face clouded with sorrow.

"Don't be so distressed," God told him. "I will bless Ishmael, too. He is your son, and his descendants will also be many."

So Abraham loaded Hagar with supplies of food and water, and she and Ishmael started out into the heat. Hagar wept and wept as she wandered in the desert. Soon, the water was gone, and she left Ishmael under the thin shade of a stunted bush. "I can't bear to watch him die!" she murmured through dry lips.

"Look!" said God. Hagar looked, and saw a well of water. They drank with joy, and God blessed her son as he grew.

## The test and the lamb

Later, God put Abraham to the test: "Take your son Isaac, whom you love and who gives you joy. Go with Isaac up to the mountain in Moriah. There, you will sacrifice him as an offering to God." A chill crept over Abraham as he listened to these words from God. That night he sat outside his tent, looking at the stars in the sky, running the dust through his fingers. He remembered God's promises for Isaac – what could it all mean? Yet he trusted God, and would do as God said.

In the faint dawn light he saddled up his donkey with numb fingers, and gathered firewood for the sacrifice. Every step of the long journey into the mountains was slow. The rocks bruised Abraham's feet, and the sun scorched his skin. But he hardly felt it.

Finally, they arrived at the place of sacrifice. Abraham piled up wood, and prepared to make the offering.

"Father?"

"Yes, son?" Abraham replied.

"The fire and the wood are here, but where is the lamb for the sacrifice?"

"God will provide that himself," said Abraham. His hands shook as he bound his son's wrists with rope, and he laid him on the wood, and raised his long, sharp knife…

"Stop! Abraham, stop!" called out God. "Don't harm a hair of his head! You were prepared to sacrifice your dear son for me – you did not hold anything back. Now I know how much you love me!"

Abraham looked up, and saw a ram with its horns tangled in a bush. So he took the ram, and sacrificed it in the flames. Abraham called that place "God will provide".

And God renewed his promise. "You were willing to sacrifice your dear son. So, I will bless you beyond measure, and because of you blessings will flow to all the people of the earth."

## A wife for Isaac

So Isaac lived, and grew, and the time came for him to have a wife. Abraham did not want Isaac to marry one of the Canaanite women who lived nearby. He wanted Isaac's wife to be chosen from Abraham's own country, so they would worship God together. Abraham was too old for the long journey back, and told his most trusted servant to go in his place.

"You must swear to me by the God of heaven and earth that you won't get a Canaanite woman for Isaac, but rather one from my own country and family."

The servant swore the oath, and loaded ten of his master's camels with gold and fine fabrics and all kinds of good things. He travelled back over many miles, until he came to the town where Abraham's brother Nahor had settled.

He found the town's spring, and waited there with his kneeling camels. He knew that when evening came, the daughters of the town would collect water. He would ask one of them to be Isaac's bride, but which one?

"O Lord, God of my master, Abraham," he prayed, "please help me to know the right girl to ask. Let it be the one who gives me a drink from her jug, and offers to water my camels!"

While the words were still on his lips, Rebecca came toward him, balancing an earthenware jug on her shoulders. She was beautiful. Could she be the one? The servant spoke to her.

"Please would you give me a sip from your jug?" he asked.

"Drink your fill, sir," she replied, "and I'll draw water for your camels, too!"

It took quite some time to draw enough water for ten thirsty camels. When she had finished, the servant gave her a glittering nose ring of solid gold, and two fine gold bangles.

"Who is your father?" he asked. "Would there be room for me to stay in your home tonight?"

"I'm the daughter of Bethuel, the granddaughter of Nahor. You're very welcome to stay." The servant gasped. "God has been so good! My master is Abraham, Nahor's brother. God has led me straight to my master's family!"

Rebecca ran home to tell her mother what had happened, and soon everyone was busy gathering straw for the animals, and food and water for their guest. Rebecca's brother Laban saw the fine new jewellery his sister was wearing and decided to go and see the stranger for himself. He found Abraham's servant by the spring.

"Why are you still standing here?" Laban said. "God has heard your prayers. The food is ready – come and join us!" So he came.

But as they sat, the servant said, "I must tell you why I'm here before we eat!"

"Tell us, then!" replied Laban.

He told them of Abraham – how God had blessed him and made him rich – and of Isaac, his son and heir. He told them how Abraham wanted Isaac to marry one of his own people, one who would worship God. "And, as I waited by the spring, I asked God to help me speak to the right girl… Rebecca was the answer to my prayer!"

"Well, that seems clear enough – what's happened is the will of God, so who are we to argue? You'd better take Rebecca back with you!"

Then the servant called for his saddlebags. As he opened them at Rebecca's feet, she gasped. For out of the dusty bags spilled fine clothes in bright colours, and glinting jewellery made of gold and silver. It was a fine gift for a bride. He also gave gifts to her mother and brother. It was all settled, and Rebecca was happy to go.

They started out amid her mother's tears, remembering Laban's final words: "Our sister, may you be blessed! May you have many children!"

Back in Canaan, Isaac was out in the fields one morning and saw ten camels in the distance. One of them was ridden by a young woman. He smiled, and started to run toward his new bride.

## Jacob and Esau

Abraham had died, and been laid to rest in the ground. Isaac was now the head of the family. He loved his wife Rebecca. Yet, like his mother and father had once been, they were childless.

"When I left my family, they asked God to bless me with children!" Rebecca said to Isaac.

"Let me pray, then, that God will!" Isaac replied. She received a double blessing, for she became pregnant with twins. The two babies moved inside her as she lay down, giving her no rest. It was as if they were fighting.

"Why are the babies acting like this?" she asked God.

"Within you are two peoples, and the elder will serve the younger." These were strange words, and Rebecca remembered them when the twins were born.

The first to be born was red and hairy. He was named Esau. But holding onto Esau's heel was Jacob. They were so different. Esau, his father's favourite, loved the countryside and was a fine hunter. Jacob, his mother's favourite, was quiet, and stayed nearby among the tents. But they did not love each other as brothers should do.

By now, Isaac's eyes were clouded with age, and he knew he would soon die. So he called Esau, his favourite and firstborn, to him.

"I know my life is coming to an end. Go hunting for me, and make me some of my favourite food. I would like to eat, and to bless you, before I die." Esau picked up his quiver of arrows and his bow, and started out.

But Rebecca overheard, and hurried to tell Jacob of Isaac's request. "You get in first – kill two goats from the flock and I will make a meal with them, and then you can take Esau's blessing."

"My father won't be fooled so easily," said Jacob. "My skin is smooth, and Esau is hairy. I'll get a curse, not a blessing!"

"Just do what I say – I'll take the curse if it comes to it…" Rebecca had a plan. She set the meat to cook, then prepared some goatskins, and took Esau's clothes from his tent. When the food was ready, she dressed Jacob as his brother, with pieces of rough goats' hide covering his smooth skin. Jacob went in to his father's tent, his heart beating fast. Would Isaac see through the disguise?

Jacob carried the food up to his father, and set it down before him. "It is Esau, your firstborn!" he lied.

"My son! You smell of the countryside! May God bless you with grain from the field and wine from the vineyard. Many will bow down before you. You will rule over your brother, and over many peoples…"

Meanwhile, Esau was returning from his hunting trip and preparing food. One brother slipped out of the tent as the other slipped in.

"Who's this?" demanded Isaac as Esau came before him.

"Esau, your firstborn!"

"So who was that, just now? He gave me food, said it was you, and I blessed him with your blessing!"

Esau fell down before his father. "Bless me, too, father! Is there no blessing left for me?"

"You will live far from the riches of the earth, and serve your brother, but not for ever. The time will come when you'll stand proud and tall again."

Esau boiled with anger against his brother. He fumed and stormed among the tents. "As soon as my father is dead, Jacob will be a dead man, too!" he roared. Rebecca heard him, and urged Jacob to run away to his uncle Laban's lands. Isaac blessed him again before he left, and told him to find a wife among Laban's family.

Jacob went alone, travelling until it was dark. Shivering in the chill of the desert night, he took a stone for a pillow, and lay down to sleep. As Jacob slept, a dream came to him. He saw a ladder, with its feet on the ground, stretching up and up to heaven. In his dream, he watched as God's bright angels travelled up and down it between heaven and earth. And in his dream, God himself was there.

"I am the God of Abraham and Isaac, and I promise you this land, just as I promised it to them. I will make your descendants as uncountable as the dust of the earth. All the peoples of the world will be blessed through you. I will never leave you. I will bring you back to this land!"

Jacob woke with a jolt and looked around. He was alone.

"God was here, and I didn't know it! This place is the gate of heaven!" he said. Then he took the stone he had slept upon and set it up as an altar to God. He poured oil on it as an offering, and worshipped there. Starting out once more, he left his homeland, his promised land, far behind.

## Leah and Rachel

On and on Jacob travelled, until he came close to his mother's family lands. He rested by a well, where he met some shepherds.

"Do you know Laban, Nahor's grandson?" he asked.

"Know him? Of course! In fact, here comes his daughter Rachel now!" When Jacob saw her, his heart leaped, and he rolled away the great stone from the top of the well so that she could draw cool water for her flocks. Then he went up to her and kissed her, and began to weep aloud.

"I am Rebecca's son!" he told her, and she ran to fetch her father.

"My flesh and blood! My dear Rebecca's son! Come and stay with me," Laban said. And so Jacob stayed, helping his uncle with his flocks.

"You're a hard-working man – it's not right you should do all this for nothing!" said Laban one evening. "Tell me, how shall I pay you?"

"I'll work seven years for your daughter Rachel's hand in marriage."

"Agreed!" said Laban. Jacob had loved Rachel from the first moment he saw her, and the seven years were like a few days for him.

When the seven years were up, there was a great wedding feast. Rachel had an elder sister, Leah, who had not yet married. So, at the end of the feast, Laban led Leah into Jacob's tent, dressed in Rachel's bridal clothes and a heavy veil. When first light came, Jacob saw the wrong sister was in his tent. He stormed up to Laban.

"What have you done? I worked so hard for you and you've tricked me!"

"Come, now!" replied Laban in a smooth voice. "It's our custom to marry off the elder daughter first. You can have the younger one too, in return for seven years' more work." So Jacob and Rachel married the following week, and Jacob worked seven more years for her.

## The call of home

It was not easy for Leah – the unloved, elder sister. But God saw her distress, and blessed her with children. Rachel was greatly loved but childless, and jealousy sparked and smouldered between the sisters. But in time, Rachel's prayers were answered, and she had a son, Joseph. Later she had a second son, Benjamin.

By now, it had been many years since Jacob had run from his promised land. The longing for home was strong in his heart. He knew it was time to return.

"Let me go back home with my wives and children, and flocks and herds," he said to Laban. "You know how hard I've worked for you. Now I must go back to my own lands." Laban tried to keep the flocks and herds for himself, and there was trouble between the two men. But in the end, Laban and Jacob straightened out their differences and shared a meal together. Laban blessed his daughters and grandchildren before they went. So Jacob left in peace, and did not have to run away in fear, as he had from Esau.

For it was still there, gnawing away at the back of Jacob's mind: the memory of how he had cheated his twin brother, and how Esau had been angry enough to wish him dead. He could hardly expect Esau to welcome him home after so long. Jacob thought hard about the best thing to do.

He sent this message ahead of him: "A message to Esau from his servant Jacob. I have been staying with our uncle Laban, where I have prospered – with many flocks and herds. I send greetings, hoping to find favour with you."

When the messengers returned, they told him, "Esau is on his way to meet you – with 400 men!" Jacob's face turned pale. It was worse than he feared. He prayed to God, asking for help. He also prepared gifts for Esau.

They were extravagant gifts: hundreds of goats and sheep; camels with their young; cows, bulls, and donkeys. Each group of animals had a servant in charge of it. He sent them on ahead, one after another, to meet Esau with this rich procession of peace offerings. Then he took his wives and children to a safe place, and left them. The next day he would see Esau again, with his 400 men.

That night when he was alone and full of fears for the morning, he wrestled with a stranger who came from God. All night they pitted their strength against each other. "Let me go, for dawn is breaking," the stranger said.

"I will not let you go until you bless me!" Jacob replied.

Then the stranger said, "You have struggled with God and men and have overcome." And the stranger called him Israel, which means "God-wrestler", and blessed him before he left.

Then, as the cool dawn began to warm, Jacob saw Esau and the 400 men coming toward him. Jacob bowed down seven times, but his brother ran to him and held him, weeping. Esau had forgiven him, and welcomed him and his family with open-hearted love. "Seeing your face was like seeing God smiling on me!" Jacob said.

Now they were back in Canaan, Jacob told everyone in his household, "We're in the land God promised me now, so throw away all your lucky charms and idols of other gods!" And so they did.

God renewed his promise to Jacob. "Kings and nations will come from you. This is your land, for you and your family."

## The dreamer

Jacob's family was large. He had twelve sons: Reuben, Simeon, Levi, Judah, Issachar and Zebulun, the sons of Leah; Dan and Naphtali, sons of Bilhah, Rachel's servant; and Gad and Asher, sons of Zilpah, Leah's servant. Lastly, there were Joseph and Benjamin, sons of Jacob's beloved Rachel. Joseph and Benjamin were born in Jacob's old age. Benjamin was always precious to his father, as Rachel died giving birth to him.

Jacob doted on Joseph, too. Joseph could do no wrong in Jacob's eyes, and the young man sat at his father's side, telling tales on his older brothers. Jacob made him a beautiful coat – not working clothes like the others wore, but something fine, the coat the eldest son should have had. When they saw him wearing it, his brothers turned their backs on him and walked away.

But the 17-year-old Joseph didn't notice, and rubbed salt into their wounds. "Just you listen to this dream I've had!" he told his brothers. "We were all out in the field harvesting. My bundle of wheat stood up straight, and yours all came and bowed down to it!"

His brothers were outraged. "Do you intend to rule over us like a king?" they fumed.

Then Joseph proudly told them of another, grander dream: "The sun and the moon, and eleven stars, all bowed down to me!" Even his father was troubled by this dream, and saw the bitter seeds his favouritism had planted in his family.

"Go out to the fields and see how your elder brothers are getting on with the work!" Jacob said one day, and so Joseph went, leaving his father and Benjamin together.

 "Look, here comes daddy's boy!" said his brothers. "Let's kill him! That'll be the end of all his fancy dreams. We can say the wild animals got him."

But Reuben, the eldest, said "No! Don't murder him! Just put him in this old well!" Reuben planned to come back later and set him free. But then, while Reuben was busy, some traders came by on their way to Egypt, leading camels loaded with spices and sweet-smelling balm and myrrh. They were descendants of Ishmael, Abraham's eldest son, who had been cast out into the desert.

"We can get rid of our brother and make some money at the same time!" said Judah. So they sold Joseph to them as a slave, ripped his beautiful coat, and dipped it in goat's blood. Then they returned to their father, and handed Jacob the torn, bloodstained coat. He held it in his trembling hands.

"Not dead! Not Joseph!" Jacob fell to his knees, weeping. His grief was terrible, and none of his other children could comfort him. "I'll carry this grief down to my grave!" he said.

## Out of Canaan and into Egypt

None of Joseph's brothers dared to admit they had sold him as a slave into Egypt. But if Jacob could have seen his son, he would have smiled. Joseph had been bought by Potiphar, captain of the guard and official to the mighty ruler Pharaoh himself. Potiphar soon saw that everything Joseph did went well. Perhaps Joseph's God was blessing him, Potiphar thought. So he put him in charge of all his business and his household, and sat back to enjoy Joseph's success.

Now, Joseph was a fine-looking, strong young man, who soon caught the eye of Potiphar's wife. She came up to him smiling softly, and took his hand, but Joseph stepped back from her.

"My master, your husband, trusts me. He gives me free run of this house. How could I betray him with you? How could I sin against my God?"

The next time they were alone in the house, she grabbed his clothes and pulled him toward her. Joseph slipped out of his coat and fled. She called for help, and told her husband, "He attacked me, and when I started screaming he ran, leaving his coat behind!" Potiphar shook with rage as his wife held the coat in her hands, and he threw Joseph into jail.

# Two dreamers

Joseph sat in the dark, rat-ridden jail. But he did not despair, for he was learning to rely on God. And God was still with him, blessing him. In time, the prison governor saw that everything Joseph did went well, so he gave Joseph responsibility for the prison and all the prisoners. Then, the great Pharaoh had two members of his household thrown into jail: his cupbearer, and his head baker. Between them, they had been responsible for all the royal bread and wine. One morning, Joseph noticed they had troubled faces.

"What's the matter?" he asked. "Can I help?"

"We dreamed strange dreams last night and don't know what they mean."

"God gives the interpretation of dreams. Tell them to me!"

"I dreamed of a vine with three branches," said the cupbearer, "and when the vine bore fruit, I squeezed the grapes into Pharaoh's cup and gave it to him."

Joseph's face broke into a warm smile. "In three days, you'll be back at your old job. Don't forget me when you're free! I was thrown in here for something I didn't do. Please try to help me."

"In my dream I had three bread baskets balanced on my head," said the baker hopefully. "Birds came down and pecked at the bread."

Joseph's smile vanished. "Within three days Pharaoh will order you to be beheaded, and birds will peck at your head." Joseph was right. It happened just as he said.

# Pharaoh's dreams

Pharaoh murmured in his troubled sleep, his eyes flickering with strange dreams.

He dreamed he was standing by the banks of the Nile when seven fat, sleek cows came out of the water to graze on the lush grass. Then seven gaunt, starved cows came after them and ate them up. But the thin cows were as bony as ever.

Pharaoh sat up with a gasp, his eyes open wide. The cool linen of his bed was creased, and a faint breeze stirred the rich hangings in his room. Pharaoh turned over and sank back into his dreams. This time, seven ears of wheat grew on a single stalk. They were plump with spring rain. Then seven more grew, shrivelled by the east wind, and they swallowed up the good ears.

"Call the magicians, the priests, the wise men! I need to know what this means!" shouted Pharaoh. But no one could interpret the dreams. Then the cupbearer remembered his own dream in the dark prison cell.

"Forgive me, my Lord! There was a foreigner in prison who could interpret dreams. I should have told you before." So Joseph was brought before Pharaoh.

"I hear you can interpret dreams!"

"God gives the interpretation of dreams, Your Majesty!"

And so Pharaoh told him about the cows and the ears of wheat.

"These two dreams both mean the same thing, Your Majesty. God is warning you what will happen. There will be seven years of plenty, followed by seven years when nothing will grow. You will need to choose someone to organize food stores during the good years, so your people will not starve during the famine."

Pharaoh agreed, and he knew just the man for the job. He

made Joseph governor with full authority, second only to Pharaoh himself. He gave him linen robes and a gold ring and chain. When Joseph wore them, he looked like an Egyptian noble.

And so for seven years Joseph was in charge of the harvests. He built huge store houses and collected so much grain that the record keepers lost count. Then the River Nile shrunk between its wide banks, the floods failed, and nothing would grow. Hungry people said, "Let's go and see Joseph, he'll help!" And Joseph distributed food, collecting money for Pharaoh. Soon many were travelling to Egypt from other lands, for the famine was spreading.

Back in Canaan, Jacob spoke to his sons: "It's no good just staring at the empty pots! Why don't you go to Egypt for food like everyone else?" So the brothers started out: all except Benjamin, for Jacob always kept his youngest son nearby.

Jacob's sons bowed low before the governor. They did not recognize their brother in his Egyptian finery. But Joseph gasped, and took a step back. Were these his brothers? He would put them to the test.

"You ten are spies, aren't you?"

"No, we're brothers, come to buy food. There were twelve of us. Our father keeps the youngest by his side, and one is no more."

"I don't believe you! To jail with you!"

"We're being punished for what we did to Joseph!" they muttered to each other. "We didn't listen to his cries for mercy, and now look – the same thing is happening to us." Joseph turned away and wept.

Joseph longed to see Benjamin: his true brother, born of the same mother. So, after three days, he sent nine of them home to fetch Benjamin. He kept Simeon bound in jail, so they would have to return. Then, he played a trick on them. He put the money they had paid for grain back in their full sacks. They found the coins on their way home, and were frightened. Would the Egyptians think they were thieves?

Then the brothers had to face Jacob.

"So, Joseph's gone, and now Simeon, and you want me to part with Benjamin, too?" Jacob was torn. The only way to bring back Simeon was to send Benjamin to Egypt, and pray they would both return. But soon the food ran out, and Jacob had no choice. The brothers had to go to Egypt for grain. Saying goodbye to Benjamin was a heavy blow for Jacob to bear, but finally the brothers started out for Egypt, and Joseph's palace, taking back with them all the money they had found in the sacks.

"So this is the youngest?" Joseph looked at his dear brother Benjamin, who had changed so little. "God be with you!" he said, then he had to leave the room to cover his tears. Later, the servants served a feast, and Joseph ordered them to heap Benjamin's plate high with food.

When it was time for the brothers to leave, Joseph had his own beautiful, silver cup put in Benjamin's sack, hidden in the grain. They had not gone far when Joseph's men caught up with them, looking for the one who had stolen the cup. They were dragged back before Joseph.

"We are honest men!" the brothers cried. "Didn't we bring back the money we found in the sacks?"

But Joseph said, "The one who took my precious cup will be my slave!" Everyone was searched, and the cup was found in Benjamin's sack.

Judah spoke up. "My Lord, let me take this punishment: if Benjamin does not return home, my father will die. My father loved Benjamin's mother the most. She bore one other child, and my father believes he is dead, and still grieves for him. If Benjamin is lost too, the sorrow will crush him."

Then Joseph broke down. "Everyone leave except these brothers!" he commanded, and the servants scurried away. "I am Joseph. Is my dear father really still alive?" The brothers were terrified, remembering what they had done. How would Joseph punish them?

"Can't you see that God brought good out of what you did?" said Joseph. "So many lives have been saved because of it. Listen, the famine will continue. Hurry back to Canaan, and return with my father, and your wives and children – the whole family!"

Pharaoh told them to settle in Goshen, Egypt's best grazing land. When they sat around the fire in the evenings, they talked often of Canaan, their home. It was the good land God had promised them. One day they would return.

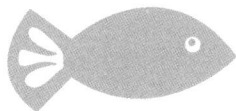

# GOD'S OWN PEOPLE

## On the banks of the Nile

Jochebed and her daughter Miriam slipped out just before dawn. They walked silently, shapes blending into the darkness. At every sound they stopped, afraid the slave masters might hear them. They crept down to the green banks of the Nile, the great river that was the lifeblood of all Egypt. There, by the trembling papyrus, they stopped and set down their load. It was a tightly woven basket, a tiny boat, containing Jochebed's three-month-old baby son. She lifted the lid and leaned down to kiss him, splashing him with her tears.

Miriam said, "I'll stay nearby and try to keep him safe..."

Jochebed slid the little boat into the reeds, and ran back to her cramped mud-walled slave house. "May God protect and keep him!" she prayed.

She knew Pharaoh wished her son dead, along with all the other Israelite baby boys. For the Egyptians hated the Israelites now. The Egyptians had forgotten how Joseph had saved them from starvation many generations ago. In Egypt, the Israelites had grown in number and strength, and the Egyptians looked at them with fear in their eyes. So they made them slaves, but they could not crush them.

In his anger Pharaoh summoned the two midwives who delivered the Israelite babies, and gave them a terrible order:

"When the babies are born, let the girls live, but kill the boys." The midwives bowed as they left, but they would not do such a terrible thing! The baby boys continued to live, and grow strong.

Then Pharaoh commanded everyone, "Throw all the baby boys into the Nile!"

Miriam stayed by the Nile, hidden among the reeds near her tiny brother's basket, and waited. Then she heard the sound of singing, and saw the princess, Pharaoh's daughter, coming toward the river with her maids. Miriam hardly dared to breathe. Would the Egyptians find her brother? The princess and her attendants were so close now. Miriam watched the princess take off her jewels and glide into the water. It shimmered like gold in the early morning light. Then the princess stopped. She had seen the basket in the reeds, and sent one of the slave girls to fetch it.

Peering inside, the princess saw the baby crying. Her heart melted. "This is one of the Israelite babies!" she said. Miriam seized her chance. She scrambled out of the reeds, and bowed down before the princess. Swallowing her fear, she spoke.

"Your Highness, shall I find one of the Israelite women to nurse this baby for you?"

"Why yes, go as quick as you can!" For the baby was crying very hungrily indeed. Miriam ran back home to get her mother.

"Care for this child, and bring him back to me when he is weaned. I'll pay you for your trouble!" said the princess, gently placing the baby in Jochebed's arms.

Jochebed's heart nearly burst with joy. She had her son back! So she sang him Hebrew songs, the songs of the Israelites, and told him of their God, and his promises, while he was a young child. She prayed for him, and cared for him tenderly until it was time to give him up to Pharaoh's daughter. The princess called him Moses, and adopted him as her own son. He grew up as an Egyptian prince, educated by the best tutors and trained to rule.

## *Moses — the rescuer*

Moses never forgot his own people. He could not walk among the carved colonnades of the royal palace without shuddering, for they had been built by the slave labour of his brothers and sisters. Then, one day, at one of the great building sites, he saw an Egyptian beating an Israelite, and anger rose in him. He came to the defence of the slave, but killed the Egyptian, and gave him a hurried burial in the sand.

"So this is how he repays our kindness to him!" roared Pharaoh when he heard the news. "We brought him up as one of our own, and now he's fighting against us, on the side of those lazy slaves!" When Moses saw Pharaoh's anger, he ran to the desert, the land of Midian, fearing for his life.

He came to a well and sat down, gasping and exhausted. Soon, seven young women arrived to water their sheep. But some shepherds tried to drive them away and take the water for themselves. Moses came to the girls' rescue, and helped them water their flocks. The young women returned to their father Jethro, a wealthy herdsman, and told him what had happened. Jethro welcomed his daughters' protector into his family. Moses married one of the girls and cared for Jethro's flocks. He learned the ways of the wilderness: where to shelter from a sandstorm, the best paths through the high places.

Then, one day, as the sheep grazed on the slopes of Mount Sinai, Moses saw something: it was bright flames leaping up from within a bush. He began walking toward the burning bush, curious that although it was crackling with flames, the bush was not being burned up. And then a voice called from within the flames.

"Moses, Moses!"

"Yes?"

"Don't come any closer. Take off your shoes, for you are on holy ground!"

Moses obeyed the voice.

"I am the God of your forefathers: the God of Abraham and Isaac and Jacob…"

Moses hid his face, afraid to look on God.

"… and I have heard the cries of my people. I have seen their suffering and felt their pain. I want to pull them out from under their slave masters' whips and bring them to a good, gentle land: a land of plenty. You are the man I have chosen to send to Pharaoh. You will rescue my people from Egypt."

Moses was stunned, utterly shocked. "But… but… I can't! Why me? What if they ask me who sent me?"

"I am God, and I am sending you. I am the God of Abraham, and Isaac, and Jacob: the God of the Israelites."

"But…" Moses was still full of fears at the thought of returning to Egypt and speaking for his people. He blurted them out to God: no one would listen to him; he stuttered; there had to be someone else for the job. But God did not give up. God promised to help, and to work miracles through Moses. Aaron, Moses' brother, would help him, and God would be with them.

So, fearful and uncertain, Moses left with his wife and sons. And, as he raised his eyes toward Egypt, he saw his brother, Aaron, running to meet him.

# Let my people go

Moses and Aaron entered the soaring splendour of Pharaoh's court to face the most powerful man on earth.

"The God of Israel has said, 'Let my people go: they must hold a festival to me in the wilderness. If they do not, there will be trouble for you.'"

"Who is this 'god' of yours?" asked Pharaoh, who was worshipped as a god himself in Egypt.

"The God of my people, the Israelites. Please let us go into the wilderness…"

"So, you slaves want a holiday, do you? Trying to get out of work again! You're not going anywhere!"

As Moses and Aaron left, they heard the instructions Pharaoh was giving to the slave masters. "Don't give them any straw – they still have to make mud bricks, just as many as before, but they'll have to collect their own straw to hold them together. If there's any slacking, hit them as hard as you like!" The slave masters smiled cruelly.

The slaves, beaten and bruised, came to see Moses and Aaron. "Now look what you've done! Call this a rescue plan?"

Shaken, Moses prayed to God for help – and God spread out his plan before Moses, reminding him of all his promises to his people, and of the good land that would be their home.

"Go on, prove it then!" roared Pharaoh the next time Moses and Aaron came before him. "If your 'god' has power, let's see it!"

So Aaron threw down his staff, and it turned, hissing, into a snake. Pharaoh summoned his own magicians, who performed the same marvel. Aaron's snake swallowed up the others, but still Pharaoh would not listen. And that was only the beginning.

# Ten blows for Egypt

Moses and Aaron warned Pharaoh of the terrible things that would happen if he did not set the slaves free, but he would not listen. And so, it began.

First, they spoke to Pharaoh by the Nile as he went down to bathe. Moses and Aaron stood by the banks of the river and said, "This is what our God says: you must free our people to go to the wilderness. If you won't listen, the river will become blood red, undrinkable, stinking. Egypt will be thirsty."

Pharaoh turned away and carried on toward the bathing place. Then Aaron raised his staff and brought it down on the water with a mighty splash. The water swirled, thickened, and reddened, like blood, and gave off a foul smell. Fish floated gasping to the surface and died. But Pharaoh's magicians could change water too, so he simply went back to the palace, unimpressed. He would not let the people go.

Second came the frogs. Once again Moses and Aaron warned Pharaoh, and once again he ignored them. So Aaron went around the land, stretching his staff over the Nile and all of the pools and ditches. They heaved and swarmed with frogs. The frogs came up into people's houses, hopping on beds, clustering together on the plates.

Pharaoh was disgusted. "Yes, yes, I'll let them go!" he said, and Moses prayed to God, and the frogs died. The Egyptians swept them into festering heaps. But then Pharaoh changed his mind.

Third came the gnats. There was the warning, and the refusal, and then gnats rose up in clouds like the dust of the desert. All people and animals were covered with bloodsucking insects. There was no relief. Pharaoh's magicians had never seen anything like it; "This is God's doing," they warned him. But Pharaoh's heart was hard and stubborn. He would not let the people go.

Fourth came the flies. "Go and confront Pharaoh on his way to his bathing place. Tell him he must let my people go. Warn him of what will happen next – the air will be thick with flies. But they will not come to Goshen, the place where my people live." God's words were clear, but Pharaoh did not listen. Soon the air was loud with buzzing, and every surface was crawling with flies – all the food was speckled with black. Only Goshen was free from them.

"Go on, then," said Pharaoh. "Go to the wilderness." But then he changed his mind.

Fifth came the animals. Moses and Aaron warned Pharaoh, but his heart was as hard as ever. All the livestock sickened and died; all the cattle, the sheep, the horses that pulled the chariots, and the traders' camels – all dead. Only the animals in Goshen were spared.

Sixth came boils. The warning was ignored once again, and Moses threw soot up in the air right in front of Pharaoh. The soot blew onto the people, and they were covered with red, pus-filled boils. The boils spread, but Pharaoh remained as hard and cold as stone.

Seventh came hail. "This is what God says," Moses told Pharaoh. "He's warning you: 'You're still building your kingdom on the backs of my people. You do not recognize my power, and so you will see more of it. I will send hail. Get everything under cover, for nothing will survive.' "

Pharaoh's servants heard these words, and some hurried to hide their families and animals. Then the sky boiled with clouds and shuddered with angry thunder, and the hail came down. Huge white hailstones bounced on the earth, smashing everything. Nothing could survive in the open – and the crops were pummelled to a sodden pulp. But in Goshen, the sky stayed clear.

Eighth came locusts. When Pharaoh's court heard the terrible warnings, they said, "Why don't you listen to these men and let the slaves go? Can't you see that the whole country is being ruined?" But Pharaoh's stony heart would not soften, and so a terrible army of locusts marched across the ground, hungrily devouring everything that had been smashed by the hail. Not a tree, not an ear of grain, was spared.

Ninth came a heavy, suffocating darkness. The air was thick and hard to breathe. Such was the darkness that for three days and nights no one could leave their homes. All sat and talked in whispers under its weight. Except in Goshen, for there was light in Goshen.

Tenth was death. Terrible, terrible were the warnings that God gave, heavy with the knowledge that Pharaoh would not listen, for his heart was set against God and the Israelites.

"This is it: get ready. After the tenth blow, Pharaoh will beg you to leave," God said. And so Moses and Aaron went to Pharaoh and warned him of the grief that would crush Egypt if he did not let the slaves go.

"This is the final message from God, your last chance to change your mind. Listen now to God's last warning: 'Every firstborn son will die. From Pharaoh's son to the son of the lowest slave woman who grinds the grain by hand, no one will be spared if you do not spare my people. When this terrible thing happens, all your people, courtiers and servants alike, will beg on their knees that you let my people go.'"

Pharaoh listened in stony silence. He would not relent.

Moses had a message for his own people too, telling them what they must do to prepare for that terrible night.

"God is going to set us free, but you must listen carefully and do everything I tell you, for my words come from God. Death will stalk this land, looking for people to destroy. Each family must take a perfect lamb, with no defects, and kill it as the sun sets. Dip a branch of hyssop in the blood and wipe the blood on your doorframe: some at the top, some to the left, and some to the right. Then get everyone inside. Roast the meat, make some flat bread, and take some bitter leaves. Then eat it all quickly, dressed for your journey. Death will pass over your homes because they are marked with blood." The Israelites trembled with fear. "As you are doing this tonight, remember that God has said you must eat this meal again when you come to the land I have chosen for you: a land of freedom, and a place of plenty. It will be your home, for you and your children. Remember."

The people of Goshen got ready to leave, and prepared the Passover meal. All shut their blood-sprinkled doors and ate silently as death came to Egypt. Away from Goshen, cold dread spread through every street, and every house. Not one Egyptian family slept, for not one family was spared. From Pharaoh's son to the son of the lowest Egyptian slave woman, the firstborn of the land lay lifeless in their beds.

## The escape

Pharaoh summoned Moses and Aaron. "Get out now!" he roared. "Take everything. Go and worship your God." Then Pharaoh lowered his voice: "Ask your God for a blessing for me, too!"

The Israelites got ready. They grabbed some food, and the Egyptians thrust jewellery on them, begging them to leave. Moses also carried the bones of Joseph so they could be buried in the land that he had called home. All the Israelites came out of Egypt, joined by many others who had turned to God. A pillar of cloud guided them by day, and a pillar of fire by night. They were led by a wilderness road, and as dusk fell they made camp by a wide stretch of water. Then, just as they were settling down, they saw a cloud of dust, and heard the thunder of chariots and the chilling whoop of war cries. For Pharaoh had changed his mind again, and ordered the army to bring back the slaves.

"Help!" cried the Israelites. "We're going to be butchered in the desert! Weren't there enough graves in Egypt?"

"God is going to save us – watch!" replied Moses. And the pillar of cloud that had led the people swirled darkly between the escaped slaves and Pharaoh's warriors. Then, Moses lifted his staff and stretched out his hand, and the east wind blew, and a way through the waters emerged.

"Cross over!" he ordered. The Israelites' first steps were slow and anxious, but then they lifted their heads in wonder – they really could walk on the path through the waters! They hurried over with their children and animals, their eyes wide, full of joy. Then the pillar of cloud moved, and the chariots began to roll once more. But when the Egyptians tried to cross the path through the waters, their thin wheels stuck and sank. The charioteers tried to pull them out of the mud as they watched Moses, on the far bank, slowly raise his staff once more. The warriors' faces filled with fear and they tried to turn for the bank, but the waters swept about them and carried them away.

# Joy!

The people of Israel stood on the far side of the water, looking back at the land of Egypt. Now they knew they were safe, and free! They began to laugh for joy, and Moses' voice carried above the laughing as he sung a song of praise.

> *"Praise God! He's our rescuer!*
> *Horse and rider have been*
> *thrown into the sea!*
> *The strong hand of God*
> *guides his people with love.*
>
> *"You lead us to your holy place,*
> *where we will live close to you,*
> *and all will know that*
> *you saved us."*

Miriam, Moses' sister, was with him at the waterside. She remembered how she had kept watch by the basket when Moses was a baby. How much had changed since those dark days! With joy, she picked up her brother's song:

> *"Sing to God!*
> *For God is to be praised…!"*

And all the women joined in, dancing and beating their tambourines.

Generations of slavery and hardship were ended. The Israelites were a people ready to learn how to be free.

# Bread in the desert

Now the Israelites began to travel through the wilderness. It was the same wilderness Moses had escaped through many years before, not far from Jethro's grazing grounds. The pillar of cloud led them by day, and the pillar of fire by night. But soon the people began to run out of bread. As they sat at their campfires in the evening, they remembered the food of Egypt.

"We ate roast lamb and bread," they said. "And those melons and cucumbers – delicious!" Their stomachs rumbled noisily.

"It wasn't all bad in Egypt!" they complained to Moses. "At least we had enough to eat. Now we're starving to death. We didn't come here to be food for vultures!"

Moses prayed to God, asking for help in feeding the people. God knew they were hungry, and he heard Moses' prayers. So Moses told them, "God will give you enough to eat. You shall have the meat and bread you hunger for. God will give plenty for everyone. The skies are full of food for you." Sure enough, that evening flocks of plump, twittering quail flew into camp and settled. Even the children could catch enough for a feast. Then, the next morning, there was a layer of dew all over the camp. When the hot sun dried it, white flakes were left behind. "What is it?" the people asked.

"This is God's gift of bread from heaven for you. Every day you will be given this bread, and you will collect just enough for that day," said Moses, and the people called the bread manna. But some collected more than they needed. When they came to eat it later, they found it was a stinking mess, wriggling with worms. "God wants you to learn to trust him for your daily bread," said Moses. "He will provide for you all the time you are in the wilderness.

You can only collect extra the day before the sabbath, so that you have a day of rest." The sabbath was the seventh day, when the Israelites remembered how God rested after he had created the world.

But, as the Israelites continued to make their way through the wilderness, the water began to run out. The people grumbled, saying "Is God with us or not? Are we going to die of thirst now?" Again Moses prayed, and again he did as God said. He went to a dry rock on Mount Sinai and struck it with his staff – the one he had used at the crossing of the sea. Bright water bubbled and gushed from the rock, and all the people had plenty to drink.

Then Jethro, Moses' father-in-law, came and found him in the wilderness, and the family wept with joy to be together again. Jethro listened with growing wonder to the story of how the people had escaped from Egypt, and he spent time watching Moses at work. Jethro saw how the people crowded on the dry sand in front of Moses, telling him all their problems and quarrels. Moses' head drooped with weariness.

"This can't go on!" Jethro said. "You must spend time in prayer, seeking God's will, and passing on God's words to all the people. Then choose good people to help you. They can deal with these daily matters." His advice seemed good to Moses. So, in the wilderness at Sinai, as they camped facing a mountain, Moses climbed up the rocky slope to seek God.

## Mount Sinai and the Ten Commandments

"I have rescued you from Egypt and brought you to freedom. You are my own people. If you will follow me, and obey me, I will lead you," God said.

Moses went and asked the people, "Is that what you want? Will you follow God and be his people?"

"Yes!" they replied.

"Then get ready to hear from God. God will tell us a good way to live." So the people got ready and waited at the foot of the mountain as a thick cloud brooded over its heights, covering it. Lightning pierced the air, and the ground trembled with thunder as Moses walked right up into the cloud. The mountain was a holy place, where God spoke to Moses:

"I am God, your rescuer. Worship me, and no one else.

"Don't make idols for yourselves out of wood, or stone, or precious things. Don't worship anything made by human hands.

"When you say my name, remember who I am. Treat my name with respect.

"Keep the sabbath, my day of rest. You shall not work on it, for it is a blessed and holy day.

"Respect your father and mother, so that blessing will be yours in the new land.

"Do not kill.

"Be faithful to your husband or wife.

"Do not steal.

"Do not tell lies about your neighbour.

"Do not look with greed at what your neighbour has. Do not let the desire for things that are not yours gnaw at your heart."

God knew the Israelites had been slaves for many generations, and God wanted them to know how to live good lives. So he told Moses how things must be done. There were laws for handling money and debts, and disputes, and for treating disease and injury. God also wanted them to know about which foods were good to eat and which should be avoided. The laws showed how they could live together, as one, under God's rule. When Moses went back down the mountain and told the people all this, they said, "We will do everything God says!"

Moses went back up into the clouds, where God told him more. Days stretched out to long weeks. "Perhaps he has died up there," the people said. "Perhaps God has abandoned us!" Already they were forgetting God's goodness and his commands. They longed for the certainty of a god you could see, like those of Egypt. So they gathered together all their jewellery, melted it down in a great fire, and forged a golden calf. But as they were dancing and feasting and shouting before it, Moses came back down the mountain, carrying two flat stones carved with the Ten Commandments. When he saw the golden idol, he threw the stones to the ground, where they smashed to a thousand pieces.

"What have you done?" he roared. "If you're on God's side, come here!" And those who came, trembling, were forgiven by God. But some of the people were not sorry for what they had done, and they died.

Moses went up the mountain again, carrying two new stone tablets to replace those that were broken. He stayed in God's presence for 40 days and 40 nights, and he wrote God's Law on the stone tablets. When Moses came down, his face shone because he had spoken with God on the mountain. And the people were afraid to look at his shining face.

## God's presence on the journey

"It's nearly time to move on!" said God. "I'm going to lead you to the land I promised Abraham, and Isaac, and Jacob. It will be your home. Don't be afraid. An angel will go ahead of you, and the warlike tribes will turn and run, leaving you a land of plenty. But you must follow my ways!"

Moses used to meet with God in a tent just outside the camp, and God spoke to Moses face to face, as people talk to a friend.

But before they moved away from Mount Sinai, God gave Moses instructions for a larger meeting place, where more people could take part in worshipping God. When the people heard God's plan, they responded willingly. They came to Moses carrying purple and scarlet cloth, gold and silver, oil and spices, rams' skins, acacia wood and precious onyx stones and other treasures, and laid them in heaps at his feet. They gave the best they had for the new tent: a tabernacle they would take with them as they journeyed toward their new land.

On the mountain, God had given instructions for making every part, starting with a wooden chest covered in gold. Inside they would keep the stone tablets Moses had brought down from the mountain, the ones on which the Ten Commandments were written. These laws were at the heart of the agreement God was making with the people, and for this reason the box would be known as the ark of the covenant. The ark was to be put in the holiest place of all, hidden from view by a curtain.

Skilled craftsmen made the ark and all the objects of dazzling beauty to be used in the worship of God. From the bronze basin where the priests could wash clean before they made offerings to the seven-branched lamp that stood in the holiest place, everything glistened and shone.

Aaron and his descendants were chosen by God to be priests; their only work was to serve God in the tabernacle. Every day, a priest was to make an offering of sweet-smelling incense, and once a year the high priest was to go into the most holy place to offer sacrifices to God for the wrongs of the people. God knew they would be tempted to forget him, and to do things that would bring pain. They were going to a land where people treated each other cruelly, where children were sacrificed to idols. He wanted to keep them safe. So he said an animal could be sacrificed to pay for the sin or wrongdoing of the people. It was a costly reminder that disobeying God leads to death, and must be paid for with a life.

God set up a pattern of worship that followed the pattern of the year, with times of turning away from wrong, and times of celebrating God's goodness – like the Passover, first begun in Egypt; and Pentecost, the festival to celebrate the barley harvest. And he told the people to keep the sabbath every week, as a day of blessing and rest dedicated to him.

After weeks of work this tent-temple was finished, with its rams' skin covering and fine embroidered lining. And everyone knew how they should worship and obey God. Then the cloud of God's presence covered the tabernacle, and the shimmering light of God's glory flooded it. When the cloud remained, the people remained; and when the cloud moved, the people followed, taking the ark of the covenant with them.

## Who do we believe?

So the whole people of Israel moved through the desert, eating manna, the bread God gave, and drawing closer to the land God had promised them. Moses called together leaders from each of the tribes, descendants of Jacob's twelve sons. Caleb and Joshua were two of them.

"We're nearly there!" Moses said. "Go up to the hill country of Canaan and scout out the land. Check the soil and crops; take a careful look at the strength of the people and the cities. And bring back grapes – they're ready for harvest."

So the twelve men started out, travelling secretly. They crept close to the cities by night, and by day rested in the green, growing valleys. They picked figs and pomegranates, and carried back a huge bunch of grapes on poles.

Word soon spread around the camp: "The spies are back, and you should see the bunch of grapes they've got – it's enormous!" The people hurried to hear their report.

"The land is every bit as good as God said. The trees and vines are heavy with fruit – just look at these grapes! But the cities have high, thick walls, and the people are tall and strong – we saw men who seemed like giants. We can't fight them!"

"No!" called Caleb over the angry murmurings. "We can take this land!" Caleb and Joshua pleaded with the people, but the crowd had turned angry and began hurling stones at them. Then, the tabernacle was lit up with God's glory, and Moses went to hear God's words.

"So they still won't trust me or believe in me? If they don't want the land, they won't have it. Not one of them will enter it except Joshua and Caleb. This generation will die in the desert, and their children will have the land in their place!"

So the people returned to the wilderness, to face the hot sun and the tribes who lived there. They were wanderers for 40 more years.

## The plains of Moab

The Israelites gathered on the plains of Moab to the east of the River Jordan, close to the land they had been promised. It was a new generation, born in the desert. Moses looked out over the people. God had said that Moses would not lead them into the land that was to be their home, so Moses spoke to them, passing on all the wisdom he had learned. He knew how hard it would be for them to remember God in the land of promise.

"Think how God helped you in the wilderness. He taught you to trust him. He gave you manna, so that you would rely on God's word, which is our true food. Remember the lessons of the hard times.

"This new land grows like God's own garden. You will have plenty – but you must obey him. Carve his words on your doorframes; talk to your children about them when you are at home, and when you walk along the roads. You must destroy all the shrines and idols of other gods. Do not exchange your true God for a fake.

"You've reached a crossroads: you choose. One way leads to blessing, and life, one to a curse, and death."

Then he called Joshua and said to him:

"Be strong, and full of courage. You will take these people into the land that God promised to Abraham. God is going before you. There is nothing to fear." Then Moses laid his hands on Joshua's head. "I am about to die. You will be full of God's Spirit to lead." And Moses went up Mount Nebo, and saw the land God had lead them to, soft and green, spread out below him. He died there on the mountain; Moses, the man who was called God's friend. The people mourned him, and then they turned their eyes to the River Jordan, and to the land they had been promised.

# A LAND TO CALL HOME

## On the banks of the Jordan

Joshua stood facing Canaan: the land he had to enter, and take. He saw the swift flow of the River Jordan swollen by harvest rains, and the distant city of Jericho on the wide plain beyond.

"Be strong, be courageous!" God had told him. "Because I will be with you wherever you go. I will never leave you. I was with Moses, and I will be with you. I will drive the hostile tribes away." Joshua held tight to the promise, and turned back to the camp.

"Pack up your tents!" he told the people. "We're crossing the river in three days."

High in Jericho's wall was a window, where Rahab stood and watched. These people, with their dusty, sprawling campsite – why had they come? She had heard how God had parted the sea for them, and how they had survived years of wandering in the wilderness. She did not know this God, but believed he was a God of power. She shuddered, and turned away.

Back at the camp, Joshua sent two good men into the land on a spying mission – just as he and Caleb had done years before: "Go and scout out Jericho," he said. "Come back and tell me what you see." So they went, and slipped through the city gates with the crowd. The guard spotted them, and they were traced through the narrow streets to the place where they stopped: the house of Rahab.

Suddenly, Rahab and the two men heard a pounding on the

door: "Open up at once!" thundered the soldiers. "The king has heard that you're harbouring spies!"

Rahab sent the two men to hide on the flat roof, under some flax leaves she was drying. Then she opened the door. "Yes, two men were here – strangers. You'll have to be quick, though. They left a few minutes ago – that way, out of the city!" And off the soldiers ran.

"I could be in trouble for this!" Rahab whispered to the spies. "But I've heard of all your God has done; we all have. I know he's real, your God of earth and skies. Will you spare us – me and my family – when you come with swords?"

"Yes!" the men replied. "Take this red rope and hang it out of your window. You'll be kept safe. But don't step outside your door – or you'll be killed!" So Rahab took the rope, and let the men down out of her window. For three anxious days, they hid in the hills while the soldiers searched; then they crossed back to the camp.

## The parting of the waters

The Israelites gathered by the River Jordan. At last, they had come to the land they had dreamed of as they wandered in the wilderness. Their parents had been slaves in Egypt, and now they would be free, with a land to call home.

"The ark of the covenant will go first!" cried Joshua. "Follow at a distance. Show respect: it contains God's Law." And so the people came, slowly, carrying their loads and leading their flocks. Then, the miracle began. The priests carrying the ark stepped into the fast-flowing river, and the water drained away to a thin trickle, blocked upstream where it swirled in a great spreading pool. Then the priests stood on the damp, stony river bed while the whole people of Israel flowed past them and into the new land. Some wept. Their parents had told them how Moses had led them out of Egypt through the parting of the waters, and now they had a miracle of their own.

"Take twelve boulders from the river bed!" Joshua ordered. "One for each tribe descended from Jacob's twelve sons. Then, when your children ask about the heap of stones, you will tell them. You will remember what God has done for you!" At last all the people had crossed over, and the ark of the covenant, the sign of God's presence, was brought up from the river bed. They were in the land they had been promised: a land to call home.

On the plains of Jericho they celebrated the Passover, remembering how they had been freed from Egypt. Then, the very next day, they ate unleavened bread made from local grain – the first from that land. From that day on, the gift of manna stopped.

## Siege and trumpets

"You'll take Jericho," God said to Joshua, "and here's how you'll do it…" So Joshua organized the troops, then began the advance. The people of Jericho watched from behind their locked and barred gates, hardly daring to breathe, as a strange army came toward them.

First came an armed guard, then seven robed priests, each one blowing a ram's horn. The eerie wail echoed off the walls as they marched around the city. Then came the ark of the covenant, carried high and glinting golden in the sun. Finally, more guards brought up the rear. This procession circled the city once every day for six days.

Then, at dawn on the seventh day, the procession marched around the city seven times. The whole of the people of Israel then shouted with one voice, a mighty roar as the horns wailed. A rumbling began, and a crashing, as the walls of the great city split and cracked and slid to a heap of rubble. The Israelite army burst through the cloud of dust and took the city. No one was spared, except for Rahab and her family. "Don't take any plunder for yourselves – don't steal from the people we have conquered!" Joshua said. Any who disobeyed were punished. Joshua knew God would not go with them if they went against God's ways.

## Spreading through the land

Joshua and his armies moved on to Ai. Once again, Joshua listened to God's strategy for taking the city. He advanced with 30,000 men, but then divided his forces. He sent a few thousand to close in on the city from the rear, while he marched straight for the gates with the rest. Then the gates burst open and the Ai soldiers poured out, shouting and waving their swords. Joshua and his men turned tail and ran, pretending to retreat, chased by the men of Ai, who whooped and cheered after them. Then Joshua stopped, turned to face the advancing enemy, and raised his spear. At his signal the second group burst into the unguarded city, and set it ablaze. The men of Ai were trapped, cut off in front of their burning homes.

Word of Joshua's victories spread throughout the region of Caanan, and the local kings gathered to plot war against him. "If we stick together, we can beat this nobody from the wilderness," some said. But the people who lived in the city of Gibeon had another idea.

The Gibeonites chose their feeblest donkeys and their oldest travelling clothes. They dug up broken sandals from their rubbish heaps, and loaded patched bags with dust and crumbs. They rode up to Joshua wearily.

"We're travellers from far away, just like you! Make a treaty with us. We've heard about how great your God is, and we want to be on your side – we can help each other!" Joshua had his suspicions as he looked them over, but he did not seek God's guidance: he did not pray.

"Yes, we'll make a peace treaty!" he said.

Soon, the people of Israel found out they'd been tricked by local men, and they were furious. "Let's attack the lot of them!" they cried.

"No!" called out Joshua. "We made them a promise before God to defend them. We'll stick to our word!" And they did.

The five local kings – the kings of Jerusalem, Hebron, and the areas nearby – heard about this peace treaty, so they gathered a huge army before the city of Gibeon and began to attack it. They hoped to lure the Israelites into a fight they could not win.

"Come quickly!" said the message from Gibeon. "We are under attack!" Joshua and his men marched all night to get to Gibeon, and took the attackers by surprise. The enemy turned tail and ran, chased by the Israelites. But a mighty hailstorm hammered them, overwhelming the armies of the five kings. So the Israelites gained their territory, too. In this way, Joshua took the land: city by city, and king by king.

So the time came to share the land among the twelve tribes, descended from Jacob's twelve sons. And the people began to settle in the land – to farm it, to enjoy the fruit of its fields. They began to live out the promise God had given to Abraham so long ago. The land rested from war, and the people smiled.

Joshua was growing old now. "Just look what God has done! He's kept his word, he's been faithful to you. Don't let go of your faith in him. He'll help you take the rest of the land, but don't be led astray by the gods of this place. You will get nothing from them. Choose who you'll follow – God, or these idols. I've already chosen."

"We'll follow God! He rescued us from slavery and gave us this good land of plenty. He's our God!" called out all the people.

## The first judges

The years passed. The people who had crossed the Jordan died, one by one. A new generation grew up, who turned away from the God who had led their people out of slavery and across the wilderness. They followed instead Baal, the nature god of Caanan, who seemed to promise fertility of the soil and good harvests.

Now, they were at the mercy of their enemies. They were kicked about and beaten, but God did not abandon them. He sent leaders, known as judges, to rescue the people. For a while, the people would draw close to God again, but then when trouble passed, they fell back, their faith ebbing away.

There was Othniel, son of Caleb's younger brother, who defeated the king of Mesopotamia.

Then came Ehud. Eglon, the king of Moab, had defeated the Israelites and ruled them for 18 years. He lived lavishly on the tribute money the Israelites paid, and grew vastly fat. One day, Ehud himself brought the tribute money to Eglon, and set it down at his feet, bowing low before the king with a short sword hidden in his clothes. Suddenly Ehud stood up and plunged the sword into Eglon. The whole sword, blade and hilt, was swallowed up as Eglon's fat belly closed over it. After that, the Moabites were defeated, and the Israelites lived in peace.

Deborah was a prophet of great wisdom, who sat under a palm tree in the hills of Ephraim. The people came to her with their disputes, and she saw that justice was done. She gave instructions to the generals, and when they listened to her, they defeated their enemies.

After Deborah's time the people drew back from God once more, and once more enemies came to crush them. This time it was the Midianites, a tribe from the wilderness.

## God's hero

As the Midianites roamed the land, swords drawn, the Israelites took to the hills, living in hiding. When they tried to plant their crops, the troops would come and destroy them. When they tried to graze their flocks, the soldiers rode at them and scattered them. They were like a dark swarm of locusts over the land, and the people, hollow with hunger, called out to God for help.

Gideon had gathered some grain from the ruined fields, and was trying to thresh it against the stone floor in a wine press. God's angel came to him and said, "God is with you, mighty warrior!"

But Gideon had some questions. "With me? Well, if that's so, why has all this happened to us? Our parents and grandparents told of a mighty God of miracles. So why isn't God saving us?"

God gave him an unexpected answer. "You go and save Israel from the Midianites. I will be with you: you will be strong enough."

"But…" Gideon hesitated. Perhaps he had misunderstood. So he asked God for a sign. "If I am to go," he said, laying a lamb's fleece on the ground, "let this fleece be soaked with dew in the morning – the ground dry, but the fleece wet." And it was. "Please be patient," said Gideon. "If I really am to go, allow me one more test. This time, let the ground be wet, but the fleece dry." And the next morning, it was.

A huge army gathered around Gideon at the spring of Harod, ready to fight for the land. "This won't do!" said God. "You have too many men. You'll defeat the Midianites easily, and everyone will say it's because of your army. I want the people to know that I am their rescuer. The army must be smaller."

"Anyone who doesn't want to fight is free to leave!" Gideon called out, and 22,000 men turned for home. This left 10,000.

"Still too many!" The 10,000 were ordered to go to the stream to drink. Most kneeled, and put their faces to the stream. Others, about 300, scooped up water in their hands and drank. "I'll use the 300," said God. "Send the rest home!" And so they went, shaking their heads at this young man's lack of strategy.

That night, unable to sleep, Gideon slipped down into the enemy camp. Through the canvas, he could see the dark silhouette of two soldiers against the lamplight. "In my dream," said one, "a huge loaf of bread rolled down into camp so fast it knocked over the tent!"

"That's a bad sign," whispered his companion. "It means Gideon is going to knock us flat!"

Then Gideon was sure God had given them victory. He summoned his men, giving each a flaming torch and a clay jar to cover it. They slipped trumpets into their belts, and then they surrounded the camp. "Now!" bellowed Gideon, and they blew the trumpets and smashed the jars, sending hot light blazing around the camp.

"A sword for God and for Gideon!" they shouted. The Midianites awoke, drew their swords, and struck out wildly as they ran into the darkness, back toward their own lands.

What a victory! The people of Israel wanted to make Gideon their king. "I won't be your king, nor will my son," he told them. "God is the only king we need."

Yet, in time, the people turned from God once more, and worshipped the nature god, Baal. Judges came, and judges went, but the people slipped further and further away from God, who had given them the land. Their enemies – the Philistines this time – had the upper hand, and treated them cruelly.

## Samson

During the time when the Philistines ruled over the land, a childless couple heard news that filled them with great joy. An angel appeared to the woman and said she would soon have a son. He was to be set apart for God. His hair was never to be cut, and he was never to drink wine. This gift-child from God was called Samson. As he grew, so did his strength. He became a man of enormous power.

One day, he was on his way to visit a young woman, a Philistine. As he reached the vineyards near her home, a young lion sprang at him, and he ripped it apart as if it were a kid goat. Later, he went back to marry the girl, taking the same road. He stopped to look at the carcass on the way, and saw it was full of bees. He bent down and scooped out the sweet honey to eat, and carried on to meet his bride. After the marriage there was a great feast, and Samson sat at his new wife's side and asked the Philistine warriors this riddle:

*"Out of the strong, something sweet,*
*Out of the eater, something to eat!"*

They could not answer it. So they persuaded his young wife to coax the answer out of him, and she betrayed Samson. Samson was furious, and a violent quarrel sprang up between Samson and the Philistine warriors. Samson was stopped from seeing his bride again, and she was given instead to the friend who supported him at the wedding.

In his rage, Samson destroyed the Philistines' crops single-handed. Tying lit torches to foxes' tails, he set them loose among the dry, ripe grain. Fire ripped through the fields. When the Philistines came after him, and bound him tight, he burst the strong ropes and killed the guard with a donkey's jawbone. He tore down the huge gates of Gaza, their city, and carried them off to the hills. The Philistines were desperate to stop him, to find the source of his strength. Then, at last, he walked into their hands.

Another Philistine woman, Delilah, caught his eye. "We'll make you rich beyond your dreams!" the generals told Delilah. "Just sweet-talk your way into Samson's confidence, find out how he can be defeated. He'll do anything for you!" And so Delilah began to question him.

"You're so strong! Amazing! Tell me, what's your secret?" Delilah asked.

"Tie me up with seven bow strings and I'd be as weak as a child!" Samson answered. So when he was sleeping, she tried it.

"Your enemies are upon you!" she cried, and he leaped up, bursting the strings. He had tricked her.

"You teaser!" she smiled. "Really, what's the secret?"

"Tie me up with new ropes, then I'm in your power!" Samson

said. But that wasn't it, either. Next he told her to weave his hair into her loom. But all she got from that was ripped cloth and a broken loom. Delilah did not give up. She wept, and sulked, and stormed, and in the end Samson told her.

"I've never had my hair cut – not once. Shave my head and I lose my power." So, one night, when he was deeply asleep, she cropped his hair, and bound him. Morning came, and so did the Philistines. Samson pulled, but the ropes did not break. His strength had gone. The Philistines blinded him, and led him through the streets to the prison. There, as he worked the heavy grindstones of the mill, his hair began to grow again.

Then they took Samson to the Philistine temple, where all his enemies were gathered to mock him. "O God, give me my strength back!" he prayed. He pushed with all his might against two pillars that held up the temple, and they shifted and cracked. The roof began to groan as dust poured down. Then the pillars buckled, and the temple collapsed with a roar on top of Samson and all the Philistines gathered there. The Philistines were crushed, and the people could live in peace.

## Ruth – from Moab to Bethlehem

Far away from the generals and the judges, the people of the land lived out their lives simply, and quietly. But they, too, were part of God's great story.

The people of Bethlehem were hungry – and hunger soon deepened to famine. Elimelech looked at the pinched faces of his wife, Naomi, and their sons. He had heard that there was food in Moab, Israel's old enemy across the River Jordan. He decided to leave his family lands and find food.

So they settled in Moab, and Mahlon and Chilion, their sons, married Moabite girls. But then, one by one, Elimelech, Mahlon, and Chilion died, leaving Naomi a widow, and childless. Her heart was broken, and she longed for Bethlehem. She had heard that better times had come to her home town.

So Naomi started out, with her two daughters-in-law, on the road home. "But then," she thought, "these girls will be alone in my land, as I was alone in theirs." She stopped and turned to them. "Go back to your own mothers, and may God be as kind to you as you have been to me! May he find you new husbands, new homes." She kissed them and they wept together, for they had all lost those they loved. At last, Orpah said goodbye to her mother-in-law, and turned back. But Ruth held Naomi and would not let go.

"Go back to your family, and your gods, with Orpah," Naomi told her.

"Don't make me leave," Ruth pleaded. "Where you go, I will go. Where you settle, I will settle. I choose your people as my people. I choose your God as my God. Nothing will part us." So they carried on, back to Bethlehem.

"Can it be Naomi, after all this time?" her old friends asked.

"I'm so old, and broken, and bitter. Look how God has dealt with me – I hardly recognize myself!" she replied. Yet they had returned at a good time, just as the barley harvest was beginning.

The golden grain rippled under the white sun, and the fields hummed with the buzz of insects and the harvest songs of the workers. Ruth began gathering stalks of barley behind the line of harvesters, for God's Law said that the poor, and the foreigner, could glean what had been left behind. The fields belonged to Boaz, a wealthy man and a member of Elimelech's family.

"Who is that young woman? Where is she from?" Boaz asked one of the harvesters.

"That's the Moabite girl who came back with Naomi. She asked permission to glean, and has worked hard through the heat of the day."

So Boaz went up to her. "Keep to my land, work with my girls. You will be safe here. Help yourself to water when you're thirsty."

Ruth sank down to her knees. "You show me such kindness, and I'm a Moabite!"

"I've heard of your goodness to Naomi, and how you left your land to live with strangers. You've thrown yourself on God's mercy. He will reward your good heart." Later, Boaz called her over to the shade for lunch and gave her food. He told his workers, "Leave her some good grain – pull it out of the sheaves for her. Treat her well!"

That evening, after she had threshed her barley stalks with a stick and gathered up the good grain, Ruth went home with a sack full of barley, and left-over lunch.

"So much!" cried Naomi. "Where did you work?"

"In Boaz's field. He has been so good to me!"

"Maybe God does remember us! That man is part of our family – he may yet do more for us! Stick with him."

Naomi saw that Boaz looked at Ruth with more than kindness as she went to glean in his fields every day. On the night of the harvest celebrations at the threshing-floor, Naomi whispered her hopes and plans to Ruth as she helped the young woman get ready. For Naomi knew Boaz had a right to marry Ruth, his relation by marriage, according to their customs.

Ruth, smiling, did just as Naomi had said. She watched Boaz eat and drink his fill. Then, as he settled to sleep, Ruth came quietly and lay down at his feet. In the deep darkness, Boaz stirred.

"Who's that?" he asked.

"It's Ruth," she whispered. "Spread your cloak over me and protect me."

"God bless you!" Boaz replied. "I will protect you and marry you!"

So Ruth and Naomi were no longer poor and alone, but were embraced into Boaz's family. Ruth bore a son. Her eyes shone with tears of joy as she gave him to Naomi to hold for the first time. "God did not forget me, after all!" Naomi whispered as she held him close.

This son of Ruth the Moabite was called Obed. Obed was the father of Jesse, and Jesse was the father of King David.

## God answers Hannah's prayer

Hannah sat in the shrine at Shiloh, her cloak pulled over her head to hide her tears. As the priests sang, and the sacrifice was divided and shared among her family, the words of her husband's other wife stung her like scorpions.

"How can he love you as much as me? Look at all these children I've got – and where are yours? Barren, dried up, unloved wife!" And so it was every year as the family came to worship God.

"But you know how much I love you – please don't cry," her husband said, offering her the best of the food. Broken, she entered the sanctuary, the holy place, where Eli the priest sat. There, she wept bitter tears as she prayed, asking God for a child. She promised to give him up to God's service.

And God heard her prayer.

The next year, Hannah did not go with the family to Shiloh. "I'll stay here with my baby, Samuel. When he is weaned, I'll take him to the shrine and give him to God." And so she did, a few years later.

"Do you remember me?" she said to Eli. "I'm the woman who prayed for a child. And here he is. My precious son. I'm giving him to God today." And they worshipped God. Hannah prayed:

> *"God is above all, great and holy.*
> *He smashes the sword of the strong,*
> *and lifts up the weak.*
> *The well fed are empty,*
> *and the table of the hungry*
> *will be piled high.*
> *God laid the world on its foundations,*
> *he gives hope to the hopeless,*
> *he cares for those who trust him.*
> *God will set all things right:*
> *his anointed king will rule!"*

Then the family went home, leaving Samuel in the shrine under Eli's care. Every year, Hannah returned, and every year, she made Samuel a new set of linen clothes, a little larger than before. And God was good to her, blessing her with three more sons and two daughters.

## A voice in the darkness

The boy Samuel learned how to serve God in the shrine. And he slept by the lamp of God's presence, close to the holy ark of the covenant.

One night, in the darkness before dawn, a voice called out, "Samuel, Samuel!" So Samuel got up and went to Eli, who was old, with failing eyes.

"Here I am! You called me!" Samuel said. Eli stirred.

"I didn't call you! Go back to sleep!" So he did. But there was the voice again.

"Samuel, Samuel!" The boy got up again and went to Eli.

"You called, and I came!"

"No, I didn't call you. Go back to sleep." But, when Samuel woke Eli a third time, he wondered what this voice could mean. Perhaps God was speaking.

"Go back and lie down. If you are called again, say, 'Speak, Lord, your servant is listening.' " So Samuel went back to bed and lay there, waiting, hardly daring to breathe.

"Samuel, Samuel!" came the voice. Samuel remembered Eli's words.

"Speak, Lord, your servant is listening!" And so God spoke to Samuel. God said that the right to be priests would be taken away from Eli's family, because his sons had done wrong, and Eli had not stopped them. They would be punished.

In the morning, Samuel had to tell his teacher what God had said. "God is God, and will do what is best!" Eli sighed.

This was not the last time God spoke to Samuel. As he grew, the people turned to him as a prophet, a priest, and a judge. They knew he spoke God's words, which never failed. The people threw their idols away and walked in the ways of God.

# A king for Israel

Samuel hoped that his children would be judges over the Israelites after him. But they did not listen to God and, like Eli's sons, they ran wild, using their power to fill their treasure chests. Samuel watched them with a heavy heart. The elders of Israel spoke, shaming him.

"Your sons take bribes – they are corrupt! We can't have leaders like that. We want a king to rule us. We want to be like other nations!"

Samuel bowed his head. He knew it was not God's plan for them to be like other nations and have a king. For God was to be their only king. As he prayed, God spoke to him again.

"They are rejecting me, not you," God said. "They have forgotten how I brought them out of Egypt and lead them to this good and fertile land. Give them the choice. If they reject me, so be it. They can have their king."

So Samuel called the people together. "It's up to you. Just make sure that you've thought this through. This king will force your sons into the army, fighting wars for his own glory. He'll take your freedom, forcing you to slave in the fields, or to make him weapons and chariots. He'll pile taxes on you to pay for his luxuries. He'll take the best of everything for himself. Do you really want a king like this, instead of God?"

There was a pause – but it was short. Just a breath, before they called out in answer: "We will have a king, like the other nations! Give us a king! He will lead us to great victories!"

Samuel called out, "Go home, all of you! You will be like the other nations." Then, with a heavy heart, Samuel began to search for a king. But when he looked ahead, he could only see disaster.

# A Mighty Kingdom and a Holy City

## Searching

Saul turned to his servant. "Where can they have got to?" he said, shaking his head. They had been searching for his father's donkeys everywhere – the high ground, the rocky valleys, among the trees – but there was no trace of them anywhere.

"Let's go home. It's getting late. My father will think we're lost too if we don't get back soon!" said Saul.

"Wait! Isn't this where the prophet lives?" the servant said. "We could ask him."

Saul, head and shoulders above the crowds, entered the town. And there was Samuel, making his way toward the high place where he was to offer the sacrifice required in worship.

"Where can I find the prophet?" Saul asked him.

Samuel's eyes widened when he saw the young man. He knew, at once, that this was the man he had been waiting for: the one God had told him was coming. So he invited him to share the feast that was just beginning. "By the way, those donkeys you've been searching for – they're safe and sound!" the prophet said.

Later, when the celebrations were over, they walked away from the crowded town. And there, on the deserted road, Samuel turned to Saul. He took a flask of oil from under his cloak, poured it over Saul's head, and kissed him. "You are the anointed king. God has chosen you to rule his people," he said. Then, as Saul turned to go,

God's Spirit filled him. On his way home, he met with a group of prophets. And now, like them, he spoke God's words.

Time passed, until the day came when the nation of Israel gathered before Samuel. The wide sea of faces turned toward the prophet, waiting on his words. He gave the people one last chance.

"Do you really want a king?"

"Yes!" they replied. So he gave them Saul, from the tribe of Benjamin.

"This is the one God has chosen!"

"Long live the king!" they all chanted, and they shouted and cheered.

Samuel watched, over the years, how King Saul led the people. In the beginning, his victories were great, but slowly Saul drifted further and further from God. He no longer followed God's ways. His worship became empty: dust and dry words. There was no peace while Saul was king, and Samuel was full of regret.

## The shepherd king

God spoke to the prophet Samuel. "I know King Saul's finished. Don't weep over yesterday's man. Look ahead. I've already got someone in mind for the next king. Take your anointing oil and visit Jesse in Bethlehem. He has a fine, strong family of sons." So Samuel looked up, and started out. He walked quickly, eagerly, already thinking how he would invite Jesse's sons to a sacrifice.

And Jesse and his sons came. Samuel saw the eldest, a tall, handsome man called Eliab. "He looks every bit a king!" Samuel murmured.

"You are not looking with my eyes," said God. "I can see through his good looks to his heart! He's not the one."

So it was with each of Jesse's seven sons. "Do you have any other sons?" asked Samuel.

"Only the youngest – but he's just the shepherd boy," Jesse replied.

Samuel smiled. "Send for him. We're not starting without him!"

Now, David, the youngest, was keeping watch over his father's sheep on the hills outside Bethlehem. He knew how to find them good grass and clear water. As he watched over them, he sang and played on his harp. But that day, his song was interrupted. His father's messenger was running, panting, up the hill toward him.

"Come quickly! Samuel is here. Your father wants you!" So David ran home, his eyes bright, his face glowing.

"He's the one!" Samuel said, and he poured oil on David's head, anointing him king as all his tall, strong brothers looked on. David was filled with God's Spirit, and it never left him.

Meanwhile, God's Spirit had left Saul, and he was changed. A deep, frightening sadness overshadowed him.

"Music can soothe a troubled heart," said his advisors.

"I know a young man from Bethlehem – one of Jesse's sons. You should hear him play the harp!"

"Send for him!" said Saul. So David came and entered the king's service. Whenever the shadows gathered around Saul, and a spirit of darkness gripped him, David played, and Saul smiled again.

But there were times when David left the troubles of the royal court, and went back home to Bethlehem's soft hillsides. Here, too, his harp was never far from his side. New songs began to form on his lips – songs that stayed with him through his life and which he wrote down in the years to come.

*"God is my shepherd, he takes care of me.*
*With him, I rest in green pastures,*
*and he guides me by quiet waters.*
*He heals my soul.*
*He leads me on paths of goodness.*
*Even when I pass through the dark places*
*where death overshadows me,*
*I will not be afraid.*
*For you, oh God, are always there*
*with me."*

## Goliath the great

"Take this grain and bread to your brothers in the army," said David's father one day. "See how they're doing." So David started out from Bethlehem for the army camp, and found his older brothers just as the troops were lining up in battle formation, their swords clanking at their sides. The air was thick with the warriors' angry war cries.

David watched, and listened to the camp talk. He heard how the Philistines had sent out their champion, Goliath, and none of the Israelites were brave enough to fight him – and for good reason. "He's huge – he towers above us – and have you seen his sword and spear? Enormous!" David went down to look for himself. He saw the wide valley between the two armies. He saw the sun glinting off Goliath's bronze armour as he stood and boomed across to the Israelites:

"Come on, weaklings! Haven't you got the guts for a fight? Send me your best warrior. If he beats me, we've lost, and we'll be your slaves. If I beat him, then you lose, and you'll be our slaves! What are you waiting for?" And he threw back his head and laughed. The Israelites were sick with fear. No one wanted to take him on. But David saw it differently.

"Who does he think he is, anyway? Doesn't he realize that God is on our side?" Saul soon heard the talk of the camp: that his musician was ready to take on Goliath. He sent for David.

"Your Majesty," David said, "I'm ready to go and fight this Philistine!" Saul looked down at the young harp player.

"I can't let you fight him. He's been a champion longer than you've been alive!" But David's dark eyes glittered.

"I've seen fighting too. When a lion or a bear comes after one of my lambs, I go after it and kill it, however big it is. God keeps me safe from the teeth and talons of the bear and the lion. He's certainly able to keep me safe from this Philistine!"

Saul hesitated, then offered David his own royal armour. David tried to wear it, but it felt awkward and heavy. He was not used to armour.

"Let me fight him my own way," David said. So he went down to the brook and chose five smooth stones that sat well in the palm of his hand. Then he went out to face Goliath with his shepherd's staff and his sling.

How Goliath and the Philistines laughed when they saw him.

"They've sent a boy armed with sticks and stones!" Goliath shouted, looking down on David. "Ha! The buzzards will have you for breakfast!"

"You think you're so strong with your sword and spear!" called back David. "But you're taking on the God of heaven and earth. You can't win!" At that, Goliath began to stride toward David, who ran forward, loading his sling with a stone.

The stone flew through the air and struck Goliath: a perfect shot. It hit him so hard that the stone sank into his forehead. The mighty Philistine staggered, and fell with a thud that shook the earth. David ran over, and took Goliath's sword in his hand, and cut off his head. The Philistine army were shocked; they looked down at their dead champion, hardly believing their eyes. Then the Israelites let out a cry, and charged. The Philistines turned and ran for their lives, but many were killed, and lay scattered by the roadside for many miles.

David was the hero, and was welcomed into Saul's household. The women poured out of the towns, singing wild victory songs:

> *"Saul kills thousands*
> *but David kills tens of thousands."*

## Jealousy

When Saul heard the women's songs, anger and jealousy began to gnaw away at him. David fought for Saul, and served him faithfully, but Saul sent him into fiercer and fiercer battles, hoping he would be killed. The dark shadows closed in on the king, tormenting him still, but now the sound of David's harp did not soothe him – it drove him to fury. Twice he threw his spear at the young man, trying to pin him to the wall, and twice David leaped out of the way.

Yet David still won victory after victory for Saul. His name was on everyone's lips. How Saul came to hate him! But his son, Jonathan, the heir to the throne, took David into his heart like a brother.

Jonathan tried to make peace between his dear friend and his father, but it was no use. Saul would not listen. So Jonathan warned David, "Run! My father wants to kill you. And may God keep the bond of friendship between you and me, and our children, for ever." David ran for the hills, leaving his friend behind.

## Hunted

Saul sat under a wide tamarisk tree. "You think I don't know what you're up to, don't you?" he said. "I know you're whispering behind my back, plotting with David. Even my own son is helping that outlaw!" His officers stepped away from their raving king. The more he spat out bitter words, the more people drew back, and turned to David. And when Saul began pursuing David again, the young man ran to the desert with his haphazard army. David turned to God again and again, in prayer-songs, or psalms.

> *"You are my God,*
> *I thirst for you*
> *in this land of dust*
> *where the streams*
> *run dry.*
>
> *"I have seen your glory,*
> *and I know your power.*
> *Your love is more*
> *precious than life.*
> *I will praise you here,*
> *even here in this*
> *dry and weary land,*
> *and my soul*
> *will be content.*

*"You will be close to me
in the dark hours,
and I will sing under the
shadow of your wing."*

Saul had not given up the hunt. He was soon on David's trail again. A messenger ran up to the king and told him, "David's hiding out in the wilderness, at Engedi!" The king leaped on his horse and started out in pursuit, his army following through the dust. As they searched for David, Saul came across a cave. It was the very place where David and his men were hiding, pressed up against the back in the utter darkness. Saul went in to relieve himself.

David's men whispered, "Go on, kill him now! He's tried to kill you often enough!"

So David crept forward, sword drawn. But he did not strike to kill. He sliced the edge off Saul's royal robe. "Saul is God's anointed king. He will not be harmed by me!"

Instead, he followed Saul to the mouth of the cave. "Your Majesty, look! My men wanted me to kill you, but I would not harm you. I cut this piece from your robe. I'm no rebel. I was your loyal servant, your friend. I have never done anything against you. So why are you hounding me through the wilderness, as if I were your enemy?"

Saul heard these words and saw the truth. "David, my son. I've hunted you down, tried to kill you, and yet you have shown me only goodness. God will bless you. You will be king after me!"

David and Saul made peace with each other, but never met face to face again. They still had a long war to fight against the Philistines.

Then, after the great battle of Mount Gilboa, a weary messenger arrived at David's camp.

"Many are dead – Saul and Jonathan are dead, too," he told David. "Here is Saul's crown, and the band from his arm." David wept. Now his songs were full of sadness.

*"How the mighty have fallen.*
*Jonathan killed!*
*How I grieve for you, my brother.*
*How I grieve for you."*

## King David

The battles were not over yet for David. There were those in Saul's family who would not accept him as king, and fought against him. But they could not overcome David, and he defeated them.

Then, at Hebron, all the tribes of Israel gathered before him. "Even when Saul was king, you led our people into battle," they said. "We know God spoke to you, saying 'You shall shepherd my people Israel, and rule them.' You are our leader!" So they anointed him with oil, and he became their king.

David turned his eyes to Jerusalem, and saw how the Jebusites held it in their grasp. He drove them from its streets with his sword, and made it the capital city, strengthening its walls. The other nations looked on, and saw how David was uniting all of Israel under him. They saw what a great nation it was becoming, under a great king. And David continued to ask God what he should do. God gave him answers, and victories to match, so that in time he defeated the Philistines, and drove them back to the borders.

Then, David took 30,000 men and started out to escort the ark of the covenant back to Jerusalem. This dazzling, gold-covered box containing the Law of Moses had been passed from place to place after its capture by the Philistines. Now eager crowds thronged the roads, joining David and his men as they brought the ark back home.

What a procession it was, dancing with joy through the countryside! It was wild and jubilant, ringing with shouts and the sounds of trumpets and harps and cymbals. And David led the way, leaping and dancing into the city itself. Michal, Saul's daughter and one of David's wives, strode up to her wild, undignified husband. "Is that how a king should behave – dancing in the streets and shouting?" she sneered.

But David replied, "Nothing will stop me dancing for joy before this great God. Why should I care what people think?"

Then there was a time of peace, and of building, and all should have been well. But as David walked through his new, high-walled palace, he felt uneasy, and sent for a prophet, Nathan.

"Look around you!" David said. "I'm living in luxury. But the ark, the sign of God's presence with us, is still in its old tent, from the wilderness days!"

Nathan prayed, and came back to David with a message. "Your Majesty, God has spoken to me, and this is what he says: 'You want to build me a house – but I don't need one. I've been with the Israelites all the time, travelling with them through the desert with Moses, and through the land I promised them. Instead, I will make you a "house" – your family. Your descendants will always be precious to me, and your son will build my temple. Your throne will be great through all the ages. I will not forget you.' " So David worshipped God, and the ark stayed in its linen tent.

As the years passed, David remembered his promise to his dear friend, Jonathan, who had died in battle. He sought out

Jonathan's son, who had been injured and could not walk. He restored his family's lands to him and invited him to eat at his own table, like his own son.

## David does great wrong

David's armies set off for war once more. But this time, David stayed behind in his palace in Jerusalem. Late one evening, he was strolling on his rooftop terrace. He looked down over the city glowing in the last rays of the sun and caught sight of the most beautiful woman bathing. "Who's that?" he asked.

"She's Bathsheba, wife of your officer Uriah, who is away fighting." He sent a messenger to her, and she back came to the palace, and to his bed. Before long, she sent word that she was pregnant.

David was horrified, and summoned Uriah back home from the fighting. But Uriah refused to go home to his wife. Instead, he slept in the palace entrance. "My comrades in arms are camped out in the open. How could I then enjoy the comforts of my wife and home?" he said, and after two nights David sent him back to the wars, with a letter for the commander.

Uriah passed the letter to his commander on the battlefield with his own hand: it was the order that would mean his death. "Put Uriah in the front line, in the thick of the fighting. Then retreat, leaving him behind." And that is what happened. Uriah was killed. When Bathsheba's time of mourning had passed, she came to the palace as one of David's wives.

Then David had a visit from Nathan, the prophet. "Once there were two men," he began. "One was rich, with flocks of sheep, and one was poor. The poor man only had one little lamb, and he loved her. The rich man took that one lamb, and killed it for dinner."

David was outraged. "Who would do such a thing? He should be punished."

"It was you, when you took Uriah's wife. Didn't you already have wives of your own? Then you had Uriah killed! How dare you sin against God like that! What terrible, terrible wrongs!"

"May God forgive me!"

"God will forgive you," Nathan said. "But the sword will not leave your family. Death will haunt it."

David prayed:

> *"Be merciful, my God!*
> *Your love is great,*
> *and my sin is great.*
> *Cleanse me, wash me;*
> *I am crushed and filthy*
> *before you.*
>
> *"My heart is broken,*
> *full of grief for my wrong.*
> *This is my sacrifice –*
> *my broken heart.*
> *Only you can forgive me*
> *and make me whole!"*

But it was not long before Nathan's words came true. Bathsheba's baby boy fell ill and died, and one of David's elder sons, Absalom, began a rebellion. He was killed by the sword: trapped when his long, thick hair got caught in the branches of a tree as he fled on horseback. And David mourned for Absalom.

The Israelites grew strong and rich under King David. The other nations saw how God blessed them. But David knew that more was yet to come. He drew up sketches of the temple, and gathered together the finest building materials he could, knowing that it would be his son who would do the building. But David had several sons, by his different wives. He had to make a choice, and he chose Bathsheba's second son: "Solomon, Bathsheba's son, is to be king after me," he said to Zadok the priest and Nathan the prophet, "and you are to anoint him." He made sure the other sons knew. There was to be no more rebellion.

As the years passed, David felt his strength failing. His life drew toward its end, and a chill crept over him that nothing could warm. He called Solomon to him. "Always follow the way of God, set out by Moses. For God has promised great things through our family." He wrote many songs, and sang his last:

> *"God lifted me up and anointed me.*
> *I am Israel's singer of songs.*
> *God's Spirit spoke through me,*
> *his words were on my tongue.*
> *He will keep his promise to me:*
> *to me and my family."*

## Solomon

The people of Jerusalem looked out of their windows to the road that led up from Gihon. A huge crowd was on its way, shouting and cheering. The sound of rams' horn trumpets echoed off the city walls. The noise was so great that the ground shook.

"Who is that at the head of the crowd?"

"That's Solomon, riding on King David's donkey! And look, Zadok the priest and Nathan the prophet are at his side."

"What are the crowd shouting?" They strained their ears to hear.

"Long live King Solomon! Long live King Solomon!"

So Solomon, anointed by Zadok and Nathan, rode into Jerusalem and sat on David's throne. Soon, the city was filled with craftsmen working on Solomon's great palace, and building up the city walls.

One night, God spoke to Solomon in a dream. "What would you like me to do for you?"

"You loved my father; you were with him. And he was a great king. I'm so young – I do not know how to lead. So please give me a wise and discerning heart, able to tell good from evil. Help me to listen to you. I want to lead your people well!"

God was pleased. "You could have asked me for riches, and power, but you did not. I will give you what you ask. But, I will also give you great wealth. Just stay close to me, and you will have a long and blessed life."

## Two mothers

The two women trembled as they stood before the great King Solomon, waiting to bring their quarrel, their trouble, before him. One of them was holding a baby.

"What do you wish me to do for you?" the king began.

"Your Majesty, please judge between this woman and me!" one mother said – the one whose arms were empty.

"What is the problem?" asked Solomon.

"We sleep in the same house. We both had babies the same age. Her baby died in the night, and when I woke, I found her dead child lying at my breast, and my living one was with her!"

"No, she's lying – my child lives, and hers is dead!" Both women were crying, desperate.

Solomon called for a sword. "Let's divide the baby between you then!"

"No!" screamed one of the women. "Let her have it! Please don't hurt the baby." Then Solomon gave the child to the one who cried out.

"The baby is yours – safe and sound. You would not let him be harmed. You are the real mother."

Solomon saw to the root of all the problems brought to him. Stories of his wisdom spread far and wide. The countries around Israel brought tribute-gifts to Solomon, and his wealth grew. Although the people were as numerous as the grains of sand on the shore, they all had plenty to eat.

Solomon was alive with curiosity, his mind was hungry for knowledge. He studied the plants and animals, increasing his people's understanding of nature. He also understood the human heart, and wrote songs of love, and proverbs of wisdom.

*"Respect for God is the beginning of wisdom."*

*"Kindness brings blessing to the one who is kind,*
*but cruelty brings trouble to the one who is cruel."*

*"It's better to have a dry crust with people who live in peace*
*than a feast in a house full of quarrellers!"*

# God's Temple

At last there was real, settled peace. The time had come for Solomon to build a temple to God. His father David had dreamed of it and planned it for so long. Now the work could begin.

The king of Tyre's forests rang with the sound of axes as the mighty cedars of Lebanon were felled for the Temple. In Israel's quarries, tens of thousands of skilled stonecutters worked, as well as strong labourers. They cut and smoothed the stone in the quarries, and dragged it to Jerusalem. No chisels were used at the Temple site, so the building itself rose quietly, reverently.

How beautiful the Temple was! It was not large, but it was perfect in every detail. Solomon lined the walls with fragrant cedar, carved with fruit and flowers. The innermost room of the Temple was the Holy of Holies: curtained off, its walls shimmered dimly with gold. Two huge carved creatures, cherubim, stood on either side, their wings touching above the place where the ark would go. It was like the tabernacle from the wilderness days, only richer, and more permanent.

"But," God reminded Solomon, "do not forget that it is the way you live that's important. You must follow my ways in all things."

It took seven years to complete the Temple. At the time of the autumn festival, the work was finally finished. Solomon called people together from all the tribes to bring the ark of the covenant into its new home. The priests took up the ark, which held the two stone tablets Moses had brought down from the mountain. Others carried the old tabernacle, and all the vessels used in God's worship up until then, and brought them with joy to the Temple. All the people followed them. The priests carried the ark to the Holy of Holies, and placed it under the outstretched wings of the cherubim. They drew back. Then, all of Israel saw the glory, the brightness of God coming down like a luminous, dazzling cloud. It filled the Temple. The priests stopped, unable to carry on with the ceremony, because God's presence was overwhelming.

"God lived in clouds of darkness, but now I have built this Temple for him, where he can live, and be seen, for ever!" cried out Solomon. He turned away from the Temple and looked at the huge crowd, the mighty nation of Israel that stood before him, and he prayed.

"Our great God, there is none like you in heaven and earth. You keep your covenant, your promise of love. You told David that his kingdom would never come to an end.

"Will you really live among us, in this Temple I have built? You are greater than the heavens, wider than the skies. Yet may you always listen to the prayers of your people as they turn toward this Temple.

"When someone prays, asking for forgiveness because they have wronged their neighbour: listen and forgive them.

"When locusts and famine come, and the people turn to you for help: listen, forgive, and send rains to restore this land.

"When enemies come, and carry this people into exile, and the people call out to you: listen, forgive, and bring them home to this land.

"Thank you that we are your people, rescued by your hand from slavery in Egypt. But listen, too, to the prayer of the many from other lands who will be drawn to you. Listen, and forgive, and make whole all who call on your name."

Then the Temple was dedicated: many animals were sacrificed, and many grain offerings lifted up. The festival lasted a week, and then the people went home.

Jerusalem was known throughout the world. Its walls were strong against all enemies. It welcomed royalty from far and wide. The queen of Sheba came with camels carrying spices, gold, and jewels. Wealth poured in from all nations, and the people of Jerusalem were strong and well fed. Everyone throughout the land lived in safety, each family under the shade of their own vine and fig tree. For God smiled on them.

But there was danger. Solomon's grand projects came to mean forced labour for his people. And Solomon had many, many wives – the loveliest women from every land. They brought their own gods with them, and set up idols in Jerusalem. In his old age, Solomon began to worship these idols and turned his back on God, the Lord of heaven and earth.

"You have not been faithful to me!" said God. "The kingdom will be torn from your sons leaving them just a scrap – a poor remnant of what might have been – for David's sake!"

## The kingdom is ripped apart

Solomon had no peace in his old age. He was harassed by enemies at every turn. Even Jeroboam, one of his own officials, turned against him and rebelled.

One day, when Jeroboam was a young man in the service of Solomon, he met a prophet from Shiloh as he was walking alone on a country road. The prophet pulled off the new cloak he was wearing and ripped it into twelve pieces.

"Take ten pieces for yourself!" said the prophet. "God says, 'I will tear the kingdom out of Solomon's hands and give you the land of ten tribes. But I will leave Jerusalem for the descendant of David: for Solomon's son. Walk in my ways, and you will be a great king!'"

When Solomon died, the people came to Jeroboam and cried, "We turn our back on the line of David!" It was just as the prophet had said. So the people of God separated: ten tribes – Israel – marched north; and the tribe of Judah shut themselves behind the walls of Jerusalem with the tribe of priests. The land God had given the Israelites was ripped apart, and God's people were divided.

# PROPHETS AND KINGS

## *Israel and the golden calves*

King Jeroboam drummed his fingers on his throne anxiously, brooding over the broken kingdom. He had rebelled against Solomon, and now ruled over ten tribes in the north of the land. His kingdom had taken the great name of Israel as its own, and his position seemed secure. But Jeroboam was still troubled about Judah, the southern kingdom.

It was small – only two tribes – but it held the fine capital of Jerusalem. He knew his people would remember Solomon's beautiful Temple that rose above the city; and the incense, the music, the processions of priests.

"The people will soon start going south to Jerusalem to worship," he thought to himself, "and before long they will follow King Rehoboam, Solomon's son, a true king from David's line. They'll join with Judah and rebel against me!"

So, to keep the people in the northern kingdom of Israel, he began to build places of worship there. He cast two huge golden calves, like the ones their forefathers made in the wilderness. He set up one at the town of Bethel, and one at the town of Dan. The people drifted away from the worship of God. Instead, they bowed down before these golden calves, who seemed to promise fertility of the soil and wealth.

But God's voice was still heard in Israel, for his words came through the prophets. Hosea, the prophet, looked back at this time with great sorrow, and spoke of what would happen as people turned away from God:

> *"They choose kings without me,*
> *and their craftsmen make idols*
> *with their soiled hands.*
> *This calf is not God;*
> *it will be smashed to pieces,*
> *like the land, like the people.*
> *Israel will be swallowed up*
> *by the great nations*
> *that lie in wait for her."*

And he was right, for mighty empires watched on Israel's borders while they followed a procession of worthless kings. There was Nadab, and Baasha, who killed all of Jeroboam's family. Then came Elah and Zimri and Omri. Omri set up a new capital in the region of Samaria, but it was not a fresh start for the kingdom.

## Ahab and Elijah

Then Omri's son, Ahab, took the throne, and Ahab did more evil than any of the worthless kings who had gone before. Grasping, murderous, and cruel, he spilt his own people's blood in the flourishing vineyards and gentle olive groves. Under Ahab, temples were built to Baal, the nature god. And Baal's cruel blood rituals were conducted to the delight of Ahab's wife, Jezebel – the daughter of the king of Sidon.

Ahab had to be stopped. So Elijah, a prophet of God, came and confronted the king face to face:

"As surely as the God of Israel lives, there will be a total drought. Not a drop of rain will fall unless I say so!" Ahab rose to his feet to seize the prophet, but Elijah ran and hid in a ravine over the River Jordan, just as God had told him to. Here, ravens brought food for him to eat. Then, when drought spread over the land, the brook dried up, and a poor widow took him into her home. God provided food for them and for the woman's only child, a son.

But the son fell ill. He grew worse and worse, and then his breath left him. His mother cried out in her grief.

"Give your son to me," Elijah said. And he took him upstairs and laid him on the bed. Three times he prayed earnestly to God: "O God, breathe the breath back into his body!" And God heard, and answered.

Elijah brought the boy back down to his mother. "He's alive!"

"You really are a holy man of God!" she replied, holding her son close.

## Fire and rain

For three years the drought carried on – not a drop of rain fell. Even King Ahab had to go searching for water to keep his horses alive. At the end of the three years, Elijah went to find Ahab.

"What do you want, troublemaker?" growled the king.

"You are the one bringing trouble – running after these fake gods," replied Elijah. "This is what we'll do. Summon the whole of Israel to Mount Carmel. Then, order all those so-called prophets, Queen Jezebel's favourites, to stand before the people. Then we'll put them to the test, and see whose God is real." And so there was a great gathering at Mount Carmel.

Elijah looked down the dry, dusty mountain slopes, glowing in the light of the rising sun. There were so many people gathered there he could not begin to count them. He spoke in a powerful voice that carried over the crowd.

"It's time to decide. If God is real, follow him. If Baal is real, follow him. You must make your choice!" But no one answered. A heavy silence lay over them all.

Elijah spoke again. "I stand here alone, as God's prophet. And there are the 450 prophets of Baal. We'll see who receives an answer to their prayers."

Elijah set out the challenge. The Baal prophets were to choose an ox, and lay it on an altar heaped with firewood. Then they were to pray that Baal, their god of wind and rain, fire and thunder, would send down flames on the offering. Afterwards, Elijah would do the same, only he would pray to the God of Abraham.

And so the prophets of Baal began to pray. Every now and then they would stop to look at the firewood – was there any sign? But there was nothing, not a spark of fire or a wisp of smoke. So they would carry on praying louder and louder, cutting themselves with knives until they dripped with blood, for this is how they prayed. Even as the sun blazed down at midday they carried on, crying out to Baal with all their might.

"Try calling louder!" said Elijah. "Maybe Baal's asleep, or maybe he's gone on holiday!" Then, as the sun slipped low, the prophets' dancing grew feeble, and their voices cracked and dry. They had received no answer. Elijah called out. "It's my turn now!"

Elijah built his altar out of twelve stones, one each for the twelve tribes of God's people. He heaped up firewood and set his ox on top. "Drench the lot with water!" he said, so precious water was poured over the ox, and the firewood, and filled a ditch Elijah had dug around the altar. "And again!" he called out. So it was soaked a second time, and a third. Then he prayed so all would hear:

"O God, the God of Abraham, and Isaac, and Jacob: show that you are also my God, and God of this people. Give them a chance to turn away from their wrong and come home to you!" With a whoosh and a crackle the firewood burst into high flames, spitting and hissing as jets of steam and smoke soared from it. The ox was burned, the offering taken up.

Then, as one, the mighty nation-crowd of Israel fell on their faces, awestruck before God. They began to shout, "God is the only true God!" The prophets of Baal were defeated.

Then, as the air shimmered in the heat, Elijah turned to Ahab and said, "It's time to celebrate. Rain is coming!" Elijah went to the very top of the mountain, and knelt down to pray for rain.

A tiny cloud, the size of a hand, drifted in from the coast, and Elijah's servant saw it. He took Ahab this message from his master: "Saddle up and go back home now, before the storm overtakes you." Ahab listened, and whipped his horses so they ran like the wind as the sky filled with great black clouds. Then the rain fell as if the air had turned to water.

"What?" roared Queen Jezebel when she heard what had happened on the mountain. "My gods will punish that Elijah, he's as good as dead!" Elijah ran into the wilderness, where he sank to the ground, exhausted and broken with despair. But God sent him food and comfort. Strengthened, Elijah journeyed to Mount Sinai, the mountain of God. There, God spoke to him.

"What are you doing here, Elijah?"

"I've done so much for you, but now they're trying to kill me!" Elijah answered.

"Go out and stand on the mountain, in my presence. I will give you a glimpse of my glory. You will know who it is you serve."

Elijah hid in the cave and waited, full of hope and awe.

First came a wind strong enough to shatter rock, to rip the breath from a body. But God was not in the wind. Then the ground shook with an earthquake, and fire erupted, but God was not in them either. Then, in the silence, came a gentle whisper. Elijah came to the mouth of the cave, his face hidden in his cloak.

"What are you doing here, Elijah?" spoke the voice; it was God's voice. And Elijah poured out his despair and his loneliness to God.

"Go from here and anoint a new king over Israel. You will also find a man called Elisha – he will be prophet after you, and your companion. You will not be alone. There are 7,000 who have never bowed to Baal."

And so it was. Elisha and Elijah walked through Israel, now greening after the rains, and Elisha saw how God was with Elijah in everything he did. Elisha became Elijah's disciple, following him each step he took, and learning from him as the years passed.

## The two prophets and the parting of the Jordan

"Stay here! I'm going on to Bethel," Elijah said to Elisha as they were walking one day.

"I'll never leave you – I'm coming too," replied Elisha. How could he leave the side of his teacher? So they went to Bethel, where a group of prophets came and spoke to Elisha.

"Do you know that God is going to take your master away from you today?"

"Yes, I know, but please don't speak of it."

Then Elijah and Elisha moved on to Jericho, where more prophets told Elisha what was to be. But Elijah was already walking on – to the River Jordan, where a third group of prophets came and said to Elisha, "Do you know that God is going to take your master away from you today?"

Elijah walked on, rolled up his cloak, and struck the water – and the river divided before him. The two men crossed on dry land.

Elijah turned to Elisha, whose head was hanging low. "What can I do for you before I leave?"

"I want to be a prophet of God, and have God's spirit, just like you."

"That's a hard thing to ask of me. But, if you see me taken up, God will give you the same spirit."

Then, as they walked, a blazing chariot and horses of fire swept between them, separating them, and a whirlwind came and whipped Elijah up into the sky. Elisha tore at his clothes in grief and cried out, "Where is the God of Elijah?" and he struck the river with the cloak Elijah had left behind. The river divided for him, as it had for his master and friend.

The group of prophets called out, "Elijah's spirit lives in Elisha!" So God was with him as he walked back to Samaria, and as he did many miracles among God's people in the years that followed.

## Naaman from Syria

Syria and Israel were at war. Bands of Syrian soldiers swept down into Israel, killing and taking prisoners. One of the captives was a young Israelite girl, who was sold as a slave into the household of General Naaman, leader of Syria's great armies.

"My lady, why are you sad?" the little slave girl asked her mistress. For a while, the general's wife hid her face in her hands as the girl twisted her hair into thick braids.

"My husband's skin is growing worse. He has a dreadful skin disease," she replied, weeping. She feared the worst for her husband, but the young Israelite slave girl had faith.

"If only my master would visit the prophet of Samaria – he would be cured!"

So Naaman started out in great pomp and splendour: with his horses and chariots, attendants and guards. He went right through enemy territory to Elisha's house. But Elisha did not go to greet his mighty guest. He sent a servant with a message: "Go and wash in the Jordan seven times, and you'll be healed." Naaman shook with fury.

"What kind of service is this from a holy man? I expected him to pray and lay his hands on me in blessing. But he just sends a mere messenger! I could have washed at home!" And he turned on his heels to leave.

But one of his attendants stepped forward. "My Lord, if the prophet had set you some great challenge, would you not have done it? So why not do this simple thing?"

And so Naaman did. He washed in the Jordan seven times, and as he came out into the bright sunlight, he looked down at his skin. It was smooth, perfect, like that of a child. He laughed for joy, then rushed back to Elisha, opening his treasure chest wide.

"Now I know that the God you serve is the true one. Nothing else comes close."

"That is reward enough – you may keep your gold!" Elisha replied.

And Naaman went home, a healed man, knowing that Elisha's God was the true God.

## Seeing with God's eyes

Still there was no peace between Israel and Syria. The Syrians set ambushes and traps for the Israelite armies, but they failed again and again.

"There must be a spy in our ranks – passing on information!" the king of Syria said. "That's why they seem to know what we're planning!"

"No, Your Majesty, it's Elisha the prophet. He prays, and God tells him how to keep the people safe!"

"Well, we'd better catch him quick!" And so they chased Elisha down, wheeling in and surrounding him with their horses and chariots. Elisha's young servant stood at his side, wide-eyed with terror.

"What shall we do?" he gasped.

"There are more on our side than on theirs!" replied Elisha calmly. The servant looked around in bewilderment. "Oh God, let him see!" the prophet prayed, and then, the young man saw – the whole mountain side was thick with flaming, heavenly chariots that circled between them and the armies of Syria. For a while after that the Syrian armies stopped their raids on Israel, for the Syrians were afraid.

## Beggars share a feast

In time, the king of Syria forgot his fear of Israel. He mobilized his entire army, and marched on the land, laying siege to the city of Samaria. The people began to waste away, and grew desperate with hunger.

But Elisha said, "The hard times are over! Tomorrow, food will be cheap, and the market will be bursting with good things."

"Only an idiot would believe that!" sneered one of the king's attendants.

"You'll see!" came the reply.

Now, there were four beggars sitting outside the city gate: they suffered from a dreadful skin disease that made them outcasts.

"We're as good as dead here – there's no food," they said to each other. "Why don't we go and surrender to the Syrians? It can't get much worse!" So they waited until it was deep dusk, and slipped quietly down into the camp, keeping to the shadows. As they drew nearer the camp, they hesitated. They could hear no sounds: no voices, no sharpening of swords, no laughter or songs. Nervously, one of them went forward and drew back the flap of a tent: there was no one there. The four men went from tent to tent; each one was the same – abandoned. And in between the tents, the cooking fires glowed a low red – they were going out.

"What could have happened?" they asked each other, wide-eyed in the darkness.

Later, they found out. As the day ended, and night drew near, the Syrian soldiers had heard a terrible sound. It was a great roar: a sound like a huge army in full cry charging down on them with wild shouts, with the thunder of horses' hooves.

"Israel's allies are coming to attack us!" the Syrians cried. In their panic they ran out into the shadows, leaving everything behind. But there was no army attacking them. The sound had been sent by God to drive them away and to save the hungry people of Samaria. Then, when all was quiet, the beggars had arrived.

The four men from the city gate went through the dark, deserted camp carefully. Before long, they found food and drink, grabbing it in hungry fistfuls until their hollow stomachs were full. But then they stopped. "This isn't right!" they said. "Such great news and we're just filling our own bellies. Come on, let's tell everyone!" Soon, hungry people poured out of the city gates. Food was cheap again, and the very next day the markets heaved with good things.

## The Assyrians are coming!

Beyond Syria, to the north, the great empire of Assyria was expanding its borders. It swallowed up kingdoms and tribes, growing richer and more powerful every year. They took Syria, Israel's enemy, and then they turned their greedy eyes to Israel: it was a land of plenty, with a coastline and access to trade over the sea.

The people of Israel watched anxiously as Assyria drew nearer and nearer. Every day, it seemed, new rumours of Assyrian savagery spread through the land. The people trembled.

At this time, many prophets spoke God's message to Israel, warning that disaster would come on them like a swarm of locusts. But Israel's kings were not listening. They followed the gods they thought would bring them wealth – the fertility gods and Baal – and they sold their own people at the slave markets.

Amos, a shepherd, spoke of God's anger at this injustice:

> "I won't allow this!
> Israel sells people like they're just things,
> grinding the face of the poor into the dirt.
> It has grown rich by cheating."

No one listened. They had forgotten how much God loved them all – rich and poor. Hosea wrote:

*"When Israel was a child I loved him,*
*and called him out of slavery.*
*I taught him to walk –*
*held out my arms to steady him –*
*but he has abandoned me.*

*"A great wind is roaring*
*against you – the country*
*will be swallowed up, and you*
*will be lost among the nations."*

Finally, the invasion began, and the Assyrians trampled through Israel's green vineyards. They surrounded and besieged Samaria, the capital, for three years. How thin the people grew, hungry and weak, unable to fight any more. In the end, the Assyrians charged the gates, which buckled like the starved soldiers who guarded them, and the Assyrians bound the people with ropes and marched them far away from the good land God had given them. King Hoshea, who had betrayed his own people and tricked his enemies, was the chief among captives. They never returned. The land was lost, and given to others.

"Have you heard?" the newcomers said. "The people who lived here had a great God, who loved them, and rescued them from slavery, but they turned their backs on him. Now look what has become of them!"

But the Assyrians were not content with capturing Israel, and unrolled their battle-plans for Judah and Jerusalem in the south.

# Hezekiah stands firm

The people of Judah watched, terrified, as the Assyrians destroyed their brother tribes of Israel. They knew the Assyrians would soon come to their land, and they looked to the north fearfully. But they had a good king from David's family, a king who would lead them well.

Hezekiah put things right in the land – tearing down the shrines and idols to local gods, and following the laws that Moses had passed on. He listened to the prophets who warned him not to follow Israel's example. Still, in the fourteenth year of Hezekiah's reign, King Sennacherib of Assyria marched against Judah. From Jerusalem's walls, people saw the bristling spears and the sun glinting on Assyrian helmets. They heard the Assyrian field commander call out in a deep, powerful voice:

"Do you expect your God to save you? Did Israel's God save them? Don't listen to your king's lies – trust my lord, Sennacherib, instead. He's ready to do a deal with you." The commander stopped, his voice echoing on the stony walls, waiting. But there was no reply. The people were silent. They would not betray their king.

King Hezekiah took off his royal robes, dressed in sacking, and went to the Temple to pray for help. He asked the great prophet Isaiah for God's words.

"Don't be afraid. You will win this battle without a fight. The Assyrian king will be filled with terror, and he'll turn and run for his own lands," said Isaiah.

But the bad news kept coming: a letter arrived for King Hezekiah telling him that more armies were on the way, warning him he had no hope of holding out against so many enemies. Hezekiah spread the letter on the Temple floor, and prayed.

"You are a great God, ruler of all the kingdoms of the earth, and maker of all! Save us from the great empire of Assyria – we are so small. Save us, then all will see, and all will know, that you are Lord of all!"

God heard the prayer. That night, death walked through the Assyrian camp. As the warm sun rose, the soldiers lay still, cold, and lifeless. King Sennacherib was wide-eyed with terror. He whipped his horses home to Nineveh, the capital of Assyria, and never came back to Jerusalem.

## Jonah, the reluctant prophet

The Assyrian empire was known far and wide for its cruelty and greed, and the Assyrian people were hated as enemies. So the story of Jonah was all the more astonishing. This is the tale.

One day God spoke to a man called Jonah, but Jonah did not like what he heard. "Get up, and go to Nineveh!" God said. "Give them my message. I'm not going to put up with all the wrong they are doing any more!" But Jonah turned on his heel and went in the opposite direction, boarding a boat at Joppa to take him away from home, and from the words of God that filled his mind.

But as they set sail, the sky swirled with dark, heavy clouds, and a mighty storm swelled under the boat. Then, as waves crashed onto the decks, the sailors began to pray to their gods in terror, throwing everything overboard to lighten the ship. But when they went below, they found Jonah sleeping.

The captain was furious. "Wake up and pray – maybe your God will save us from this storm," he said. But still it carried on, tossing the boat like a cork on the waves. "Someone must have done wrong. Let's draw lots to see whose god is angry with them!"

So they did, and Jonah's name was drawn. The sailors bombarded him with questions: "Who are you?" "What have you done?" "Who is your god?"

"I'm an Israelite, and I worship God, who made the land and the seas. It's my fault – I'm running from God. So throw me over the side!"

At first, they would not. They tried to row for shore, but it was hopeless. In the end, they threw Jonah overboard. Then the wind quietened, and the waves smoothed over Jonah's head.

He drifted down through the waters, his clothes billowing like sails, the air bubbling from his mouth. Then a huge fish swallowed him, and for three days he prayed to be set free from death. On the third day, the fish spat him out on the shore.

Now God spoke to Jonah again. "Go to Nineveh and give them my message. I won't put up with their evil any more!" This time Jonah listened. So he went to the great city and began to preach, telling them God would bring trouble on them if they did not change. As Jonah spoke, he saw the crowd's faces turn to him eagerly. They were listening to him, and soon they began to follow God's ways. So God held back from punishing them.

"I knew this would happen!" Jonah fumed, exhausted. "I knew you were so full of love and forgiveness that you'd let them off if they said sorry. Now I look a fool, because you're not going to bring trouble on them after all!"

But that was not how God saw it. "I can turn away from anger!" he said. "Nineveh was full of people doing wrong because they didn't know what was right. I wanted them to stop doing wrong, and they have. I care what happens to the people of this great city!"

# Josiah in Jerusalem

Jerusalem had been at peace since the Assyrians had left, but its kings had slipped into bad ways: the ways of the northern kingdom, Israel, which was now scattered and destroyed. The prophets warned the people of Judah to change. Isaiah told them the empire of Babylon was looking hungrily their way. Jeremiah told them to live their lives well, as God's faithful people.

One king listened. He was Josiah, who came to the throne of David at the age of eight. When he grew up, he ordered the Temple to be repaired. Amid the dust of the rebuilding, a priest uncovered something. It had been hidden away, unread, for many years. It was the scrolls of the Law – God's words telling the people how they should live.

King Josiah listened with mounting horror as the words were read to him. "We haven't done any of this!" he said. "Not for generations!" He took the advice of the prophetess Huldah: "God is angry with this people. But the king can give them time, by changing now!"

Josiah sprang into action, bringing everyone to the Temple. He read out all the words on the scrolls. When they heard God's Law, all the people committed to follow it. Then the purge began: the idols to false gods were thrown away and burned. The terrible place where children were sacrificed was destroyed. Everything to do with false gods, however golden, however valuable, was utterly destroyed. Josiah went north, where their brother tribes of Israel had set up altars to Baal, and destroyed those altars too. The land was swept clean of all its false-god rubbish. Then Josiah ordered, "Let's celebrate Passover as it says in these scrolls!"

For the people had forgotten Passover – forgotten the meal of lamb with flat bread and bitter leaves that had first been eaten in Egypt. Not one Passover had been celebrated since Samuel's time. Now, together, the people of Judah kept this solemn feast. From then on, the people led good lives, following the laws Moses had given.

However, after Josiah, new kings came who drifted away from God, and who did not lead the people well. And the Babylonian army was marching into country after country.

## Jeremiah sees

Judah's bad kings tried to ignore the prophet Jeremiah, but he had a way of making God's messages heard. He saw God's hand at work everywhere. He watched a potter smoothing clay into a pot with wet fingers. If the pot did not rise on the wheel as it should, the potter simply rolled the brown clay up and began again. Jeremiah spoke God's words to the people.

" 'I can reform a people, just as the potter reforms the pot!' God says. 'I can make them afresh!' " But the people, and the rulers, simmered with rage at Jeremiah, who always noticed all their wrongdoing.

Then, when Jehoiakim was king in Jerusalem, the great empire of Babylon finally marched on this small land, drawn by the gold of Solomon's great Temple. The armies of Babylon's emperor, the mighty king Nebuchadnezzar, invaded Judah and laid siege to Jerusalem, cutting off its food and water. In the end, the king of Judah had no choice but to surrender. The king was taken prisoner, along with all the statesmen and scholars, artists and craftsman. They were bound and led away as captives, 10,000 of them, behind donkeys carrying the gold and bronze that had been stolen from their Temple. Only the poorest of the people were left in Jerusalem, and Jeremiah was among them. Once again, he spoke God's words:

*"A wind has blown down from the north.*
*A wind that tears the land apart – destructive,*
*bringing terrible armies in its towering clouds.*

*"I looked at the land – nothingness.*
*The land was empty of people*
*and the birds had flown away.*
*No green in the fertile valleys.*
*Gone. Empty. Desolate."*

But worse was to come for the people of Jerusalem. For once more the Babylonians laid siege to the city, poor and broken as it was. "This time, they will destroy us!" said Jeremiah, and he was right. What was left of the Israelite army slipped out of the city, only to be crushed on the plains of Jericho. Then the Babylonians rushed back to Jerusalem with flaming torches, shouting their cruel victory songs. They began by burning the Temple, the heart of the city.

Soon, nothing was left. All they thought valuable – treasure and people – was carried off to Babylon far away. So the people of Judah went into captivity, away from their land. The Babylonians left a few, just a few people, who wandered among the heaps of blackened stone. The land became desolate, sleeping in a long sabbath rest, to make up for all the sabbaths the people had not kept.

Jeremiah remained among the ruins, speaking God's words:

*"I will gather them together,*
*bring them back from faraway lands.*
*Once more they will live here in safety.*
*I will give them a gift: a heart devoted to me.*
*They and their children will be with me again,*
*planted and flourishing in this good land."*

# FAR FROM HOME

## In Babylon

It was a long, slow trek across the desert to Babylon's lands in the east. The captives walked with bowed heads. They could not bear to look back toward the smoking ruins of Jerusalem, their blackened home. Their feet ached, but their hearts ached more. At last they reached those mighty rivers, the Tigris and the Euphrates, that snaked through Babylon's green plains. There, they rested their dusty feet.

> *"We sat down*
> *by the waters of Babylon*
> *and wept to think of*
> *our home, Jerusalem.*
> *We could not sing*
> *when our captors*
> *called for songs.*
> *On the branches*
> *of the poplars*
> *we hung up our harps;*
> *how could we sing*
> *our songs of home*
> *in this strange land?"*

And as they thought of Jerusalem, there was one among its ruins who remembered them, too. The prophet Jeremiah, who had been left behind, wrote to them. "You must settle down in Babylon. Build houses and plant gardens, have children, for your stay will be long. Pray for the cities where you live, and work for their good."

So they settled far from home. As they sat by their new firesides, and walked along the unfamiliar roads, they taught each other God's laws, and were comforted by listening to the great stories from their history. They remembered how they had been God's people in the past, and how he had helped them.

As they did so, their belief that they were still God's people grew stronger. And it was at this time, when they were far from home, that the exiles from Judah became known as the Jews.

## Ezekiel hears God's promises

Ezekiel, the young prophet and priest, was one of the many thousands who had been taken captive in Jerusalem's rubble and carried away to Babylon. There, so far from home, he was called to speak God's word to all the lost, heartbroken exiles. For God had not abandoned them.

"My people are like sheep," God told them through the prophet. "They have been frightened, and scattered over the rocky hillsides. Their old shepherds did not care for them, so I will do it myself. I'll go and find all the lost ones and bring them back. I will restore their land – the grass will be green again, and the trees will blossom with the promise of fruit. I'll heal those who are sick and hurt, and I will choose one to care for my whole flock, a shepherd king like David. They will live together in peace, and they will be my pride and joy."

But, despite these promises, the exiles found it hard to live in hope, for they had lost heart.

## The dry bones will live again

Ezekiel spoke God's words to the exiles. "You did wrong in your own land, the land I gave you, and everything became sour and spoiled because of it. Now, when I gather you back together, it will be different. You will be washed clean, and given a new heart, and a new spirit. Then, you will live well. You will be my people, and I will be your God." And God gave Ezekiel a vision of how this would be.

Ezekiel saw a dry and barren plain under a blistering sun, and lying in the dust were scattered heaps of white bones. He stepped among them carefully. They were human bones.

"Can these bones live?" God asked.

"You are God – only you can say!"

"Then I say – prophesy over these bones, and you will see them live!"

So Ezekiel spoke out over dust and bones, telling them to listen to the word of God. As he spoke, a strange sound echoed across the plain. The bones were rattling and clanking, coming together. Then flesh formed on the bones, and skin appeared. The plain was covered with lifeless bodies, with no breath in them.

"Prophesy again! Tell breath to come from the four winds – from the north, the south, the east, and the west. Breathe life into the lifeless!"

And that is what Ezekiel did. The winds came, and the lifeless ones gasped with one echoing gasp as their breath returned. They rose to their feet as a great nation.

Then God explained, "My people say they are dried up like these bones, and that they have no hope. But I will bring them back home alive. They will be one nation again in the land I promised them long ago. They will be loyal to me, and I will give them a great leader, one like King David – a leader who will be Prince of Peace for ever!"

At these words, some among the exiles turned to look back along the dusty road home with a new light in their eyes. It was the light of hope.

## Daniel and the king

Mighty Nebuchadnezzar, king of Babylon, spoke to his chief official. "Look among the exiles, and pick out the cleverest and strongest of them all. Select those who are of noble birth, handsome, and quick to learn. Then train them for my service. My empire grows, and the burden of leadership is heavy on me."

Among those the chief official picked were Daniel, Shadrach, Meshach, and Abednego. They began at the beginning, learning the way the Babylonians formed their writing by cutting into soft clay tablets. Soon, they were reading Babylonian poetry and mythology, and studying their medicine and astrology. But, in all this, they did not forget the God of their people. When they were offered delicacies from the king's own table, they refused them. They would not break the food laws Moses gave in the desert. The Babylonians were astonished to see them growing so strong, looking so healthy, on their simple diet of vegetables and water.

The three years' training soon passed, and all the young students were summoned to stand before Nebuchadnezzar so he could question them. The great king was astonished by the wisdom of Daniel, Shadrach, Meshach, and Abednego: it was far above that of his own magicians and enchanters. And Daniel was wisest of them all.

One night, when all were sleeping, and only the faintest of lamps flickered in the palace, the king sat up with a gasp, trembling and shaking. Try as he might, he could not get back to sleep. Every time he shut his eyes, the strange dream returned.

"Tell me what it means!" he commanded his magicians and fortune-tellers.

"Your Majesty, tell us the dream, and we will interpret it!" They bowed low to the ground.

"No!" roared the king. "You must tell me what I dreamed, and then interpret it!"

"Impossible! Only the gods could do that!"

The king was so enraged that he ordered all the wise men in the land to be killed. And that included Daniel. When he heard, Daniel walked right up to the raving king. The king quietened, and turned to Daniel. Bowing low, Daniel spoke.

"Give me time, Your Majesty, and I will interpret your dream!"

The king nodded, and dismissed him with a wave of his hand. Daniel and his friends prayed through the long night, until Daniel saw the dream and its meaning. For God had given him insight into the meaning of dreams and visions.

"Thank you, God – you are wise beyond wisdom," he prayed. "Things hidden in darkness are seen by you, for you are light. You have made known to me the dream of the king!"

So, that morning, Daniel approached the royal throne.

"You dreamed of a great, dazzling statue, with a head of pure gold, and all of it shining with burnished metal – all except its feet, which were clay mixed with iron. Then the statue was struck hard on its feet by a great rock, and the statue buckled and fell. It means that, mighty as you are, your rule will end, and another empire will come after you. Finally that empire will fall too…"

The king stood up, astonished. He gave Daniel and his friends great power and wealth in the land, and authority over all the new wise men and sorcerers the king had appointed. At this, a faint jealous murmur began to ripple through the glittering court.

## Four shadows in the fire

The great king of Babylon, who had wealth and power beyond description, called his finest goldsmiths together.

"Make a mighty gold statue, tall enough for all the crowds to see. Then tell my subjects to worship it!" he said. The goldsmiths backed away from the royal throne, bowing as they left.

How the eyes of the Babylonian wise men glinted when they heard the king's plan! "This could be our chance to stop those exiles from Judah – the Jews. They will never worship a statue, an idol! And then the king will punish them." The Babylonians' whispers were twisted with envy, for the king had given the foreigners fine robes of office and chests full of gold.

When the goldsmiths had finished their work, the tall gold statue was raised up on the wide plain near the city. And the king's officials were gathered together to worship it. Then the ceremony began, and the air was filled with the music of flutes, and horns, and lyres. All bowed down before Nebuchadnezzar's statue; all except Shadrach, Meshach, and Abednego. They turned their backs on the idol, and would not worship it. The Babylonian wise men hurried eagerly to tell the king, who summoned them to his presence. The three young men drew near the great king and stood tall despite their fear.

"Is this true? You won't worship my statue? You know what will happen – you'll be thrown into a blazing, fiery furnace!" he roared.

"We mean you no disrespect, but we will not worship your god, or bow down to a gold statue. We will only worship the true God. He can save us if he wishes, but whether he will or not, we cannot go against him."

And so the three men were bound with tight, strong ropes. The door of the furnace was opened. The blast of heat was so great that it killed the guards who threw them forward, and Shadrach, Meshach, and Abednego fell down into the white hot flames. King Nebuchadnezzar watched them; they were dark shadows among the bright flames. As he did so, he gasped, and jumped to his feet, pointing a trembling finger at the furnace.

"There were three men thrown in, weren't there?"

"Certainly, Your Majesty!"

"So why can I see four figures… walking around, unbound, unharmed? And the fourth – he looks like an angel!" The king then spoke loud and clear. "Servants of the true God, come out!" And out the three came. Not a hair of their heads, not a thread of their clothes, was singed.

"Praise be to your God, who sent an angel to save you! He is the true God!"

## The writing on the wall

Time passed, and the mighty King Nebuchadnezzar died. His son, Balshazzar, now ruled in his place. The new king gave a great feast for thousands of nobles, and the wine flowed freely. As Balshazzar was drinking, he remembered the beautiful, sacred goblets his father had taken from the Temple in Jerusalem.

"Bring those Jewish goblets from the treasury, and fill them up!" he ordered.

The golden cups that had been used in Temple worship were passed between the drunkards, who raised a toast to their idols of gold and silver, wood and stone. "To our gods!" they called in their slurred voices.

Then, as they watched in horror, writing appeared on the wall. Balshazzar's blood drained from his face and he trembled. No one could understand what the writing said, not one of the wise men. But the queen remembered Daniel, who could interpret many things, and he was summoned to the feast. He looked at the words:

*MENE MENE TEKEL PARSIN*

"This is what the words mean: 'number, number, weight, divisions'." Daniel looked out over the hushed court, and then turned back to the king. "This is what it means for you: God has counted your days – your rule will come to an end. You have been placed on the scales, and have been found lightweight. Your kingdom will be divided between the Medes and the Persians."

That very night, Balshazzar was killed, and Darius, great ruler of the Medes and Persians, seized the throne and all Balshazzar's lands. Once more, the mighty empires were changing at the point of a sword.

# The den of lions

Whatever Daniel did he did well, and the new king Darius saw that he was wiser than anyone else in the land. So Daniel was given power over all the kingdom. Others in the court, however, watched him with bitter, jealous hearts, waiting for him to make a mistake. "We won't catch him out – not unless it's something to do with his God!" they grumbled; and the grumbles turned to plotting. They went to see the king.

"Your Majesty, may you live for ever!" they began. "Pass a law of the Medes and Persians – which can never be undone – to say that all your subjects must pray to you for 30 days. Anyone who breaks the law will be thrown to the lions!" Now, the king was flattered by this idea and did as they suggested.

When Daniel heard this, he went home – to an upstairs room where the windows faced the desert, and Jerusalem far away. There, he prayed. He prayed to God three times a day, just as he had always done.

Soon the king was told of his disobedience, and gave the order: "Throw him to the lions!" Then he turned to Daniel, his trusted advisor, with a sigh. Darius did not wish him dead, but even a king could not change the law. "May your God rescue you!" he said sadly.

So Daniel was thrown into the lions' den, and a stone was rolled across the entrance. The stone was sealed, and Darius and all his noblemen pressed their signet rings into the wax. No one would break that seal; no one could rescue Daniel.

That evening, the king sent away his musicians and dancers, and he left his fine food untouched. The night seemed long as he paced the marble floors, watching for dawn. At first light, he hurried to the den.

"Daniel, has your God saved you?" he called out.

"Your Majesty! My God sent an angel to shut the mouths of the lions, because I never did you wrong!"

The king's face softened into a smile. "Get him out right away!" he ordered. "And those who plotted against him can be the lions' breakfast!"

So Darius, too, came to believe in God. He wrote to all the peoples in his empire proclaiming how Daniel's God was mighty and powerful, and how God had saved Daniel from the lions.

So Daniel continued to do good in the court of the king, but he still longed for his home. He read the writings of Jeremiah again and again, praying over their promise that God would bring his people back to Jerusalem. He continued to be a man of visions and dreams, who listened to God's word and spoke with angels. He lived into the time of Cyrus, the great Persian king who became emperor of Babylon. And Cyrus began to look kindly on the Jewish people. At last, there was hope.

## Home

So Cyrus, the king of Persia, now ruled. His mighty empire spread across deserts and plains, fertile valleys and mountains. It reached as far as the small land of Israel in the west. And Cyrus released the Jewish exiles to go home. As his proclamation rang out, they began gathering their belongings together quickly, with joy in their hearts. For this is what the king said:

"God has given me a mighty empire, and has chosen me to build a Temple for him in Jerusalem. His people are freed to go home and begin this great work!"

Cyrus opened his treasury and heaped on them the 5,400

precious golden things that had been taken from the old Temple. Nearly 50,000 people started out – a great exodus, back to their old family lands, where they settled once more. They started to rebuild. They began with the altar at the heart of the Temple, offering sacrifices to God on the first day of building. As the foundations were laid, they sang once more the songs of King David. But their shouts and songs of joy mingled with the weeping of the old priests, who remembered the terrible burning of the old Temple.

Soon, though, the work slowed, and the dreams of a new beginning faded. Squabbles broke out among the builders, and enemies looked jealously on as the Jews reclaimed their old lands. For Judah had not been empty during the exile. They took their claim to the land to the Persian rulers: to Cyrus, and Xerxes, and the kings after them, stirring up opposition to the rebuilding.

In time, the builders lay down their tools and walked away from the ruins. But God did not give up, and sent prophets to encourage them. Zechariah had visions of a man measuring out a new, blessed Jerusalem, a home for all who had been scattered.

At last the Temple was finished, and the returned exiles tried to worship again; but many of their people were still so far away, across the desert, and the land felt empty and desolate without them.

## Queen Esther

Many of the Jewish people had been scattered since their land fell, like seeds blown before the wind. Mordecai found himself living in exile in the Persian city of Susa. There, he shared his home with his cousin, Esther, who was an orphan. Mordecai had brought her up, loving her as his own child. This was in the time when Persia, and the great King Xerxes, ruled all the lands from Cush in the south to India in the east. It was the mightiest empire in the world, and Susa was its capital.

The whole of the city was busy and bustling, for King Xerxes was having a feast for all the princes, nobles, and people of the city. His walled gardens were the perfect setting, with their mosaics of mother of pearl and rich, shining stones, and their silver columns and couches.

When the king had been feasting and drinking for seven days, he said, "My queen, Vashti, is the most beautiful woman you will ever see – order her to come here, so we can all look at her!" Now, the queen had no wish to be paraded before her husband's drunken guests like a common dancing girl, and she did the unthinkable – she disobeyed a direct order from the king. He raged against her and had her thrown into exile.

Soon, the king began to regret that he had no queen, and his lands were searched for the most beautiful young women so he could chose one for his new bride. Many were brought to the palace – and Esther was among them, for she had grown in grace and loveliness. They went to the harem, the women's quarters, where they were given fine food and soothed with rich oils and perfumes. During the months that Esther was in the harem, Mordecai would stroll along outside, to see her or to hear news of her.

The time came for Esther to be presented to the king. As she entered the throne room, a murmur went around the court. She was loveliness itself, and the king chose her for his queen. The king did not just admire her beauty, he adored her, and gave her a royal crown, honouring her above all. But she never told him she was a Jewish exile.

# Plotting

Mordecai sat at the king's gate with all the other royal officials, discussing matters of state importance. He was proud that he had been made one of the king's officials. As he sat and joined in with the serious conversation, he always listened for any news of Esther.

One day, he heard something quite different, something that chilled his blood. For two officers who guarded the doorway were talking angrily against the king. They were plotting his murder. When Mordecai heard of it, he hurried to Queen Esther, who told the king of Mordecai's warning. Mordecai's actions were faithfully written down in the record of the king's reign, but nothing was done to reward him.

Now, Haman was second in command of the kingdom, and all the officials at the king's gate bowed down before him; all except one: Mordecai. Day after day he refused, and day after day Haman's anger grew. When he found out Mordecai was a Jew, he hatched a plot to kill him and all the Jews in the empire. He persuaded the king that the Jews were disloyal, not keeping to Persia's laws and customs. So the king wrote a terrible law, to be taken from the capital to the furthest provinces. The king sealed it with his ring, making it binding. The law stated that all Jews, young and old, men and women, should be killed on the thirteenth day of the twelfth month. All of Susa was horrified by this barbarous plan.

Mordecai was shocked to see the evil that was growing out of his quarrel with Haman. He put on sackcloth and covered his head with ashes in his grief, and filled the city streets with cries for his people. The queen longed to help, but she was fearful, because she had kept her faith secret. What is more, the king had not sent for her for many days. How could she approach him to appeal for her people when she had not been sent for? To do so would risk death.

But Mordecai sent her a message. "You can't hide that you are a Jew for ever," he said. "But who knows, maybe you were made queen for this moment, to save your people!"

So Esther gathered her courage, and asked the Jewish exiles to fast and pray for her as she made her approach to the king. She dressed in her royal robes and went and stood in the inner court of the palace, within sight of Xerxes' throne. The king smiled when he saw his wife, and extended his gold sceptre toward her, signalling that she should draw near.

"What is your request, my queen? I will give you anything, even half my kingdom!"

"I have prepared a banquet for you and for Haman – my request is that you come!" And so they did.

While they were eating, the king asked again, "My queen, what is it you would like me to do for you? Name it and it is done!"

"Tomorrow, I will hold another banquet for you and Haman. Please come, and then I will tell you."

But Haman was still seething with fury toward Mordecai. Haman built a high gallows that loomed over his house, and he planned to ask the king's permission to hang Mordecai the very next day. But that night, the king could not sleep. He ordered his ministers to fetch the records of his reign, and they read to him in the lamplight. Their voices lilted on through the night and into the morning until the king called out, "Stop! Read that again!" It was the record of Mordecai's discovery of the plot to kill the king.

"What was done to reward Mordecai?" said the king. His ministers searched through the records.

"Nothing, Your Majesty!" they replied. "We find no record of any reward."

"Well, something should be done. Who is in the court?" the king demanded.

"Haman, Your Majesty." For Haman had come to ask permission to hang Mordecai.

"Bring Haman in at once!" The king looked at Haman. "What should be done for a man the king wishes to reward?" Haman bowed low, a smile creeping across his face. He thought the king was going to reward him, so he spoke of all the honours he wished for himself.

"Let the man you wish to reward wear the king's robe and ride the king's horse through the streets. And let a herald announce to all the people that this is the man the king honours!" Haman's eyes lit up as he imagined himself riding in state on the king's horse, admired by all the people.

"Go and fetch Mordecai," ordered the king. "He is the man I wish to honour. You spoke well of how I should treat such a man. Arrange Mordecai's reward yourself!" Haman gasped, shocked, but he had to obey the king.

So it was Haman who set Mordecai on the king's horse and draped him in the king's robe. It was Haman who played the part of Mordecai's herald: leading the horse through the crowded streets, and announcing to all that Mordecai was the man the king honoured. When the task was done, Haman hurried home with his head covered, filled with shame.

Then, that evening, when the king and Haman were at Esther's banquet, the king asked Esther, "Tell me your request, and I will grant it!"

Esther saw the kind look in his eyes, and began, "Oh Your

Majesty, I and my people have been sentenced to death. Please spare us!"

"Who has dared to do such a thing?" The king's face clouded with anger.

"Haman, who sits at your side!"

The king's goblet clattered to the floor as he rose to his feet, furious. Haman grabbed Esther, begging for mercy, but the king roared, "How dare you lay your hands on the queen!"

Then, in the silence, one of the attendants stepped forward and said, "A gallows has been built at Haman's house. He wanted to hang Mordecai from it!"

"He can hang from it himself!" growled the king, tearing the ring of authority from Haman's finger. But that was not the end of the matter, for the Jews were still under sentence of death. Esther fell down at the king's feet, sobbing.

"Please overrule this terrible order to kill all the Jews! There is not much time! How can I bear to see the destruction of my people, my family?"

"I cannot undo the law that has been passed, but something can still be done. I can give the Jews the right to defend themselves. Mordecai can write orders as you both see best, and I will seal them with my ring. It will be as you wish! I also give you Haman's lands, and Mordecai will have all his authority."

So the orders were written, and the king's messengers rode their swiftest horses through the land. For it was nearly time for the killing to begin. Wherever the messengers went, they brought great joy, spreading through the empire until all the Jews heard and gathered to defend themselves. No one could stand against them.

Now that Mordecai had authority in the land, the Jews had all their rights restored. And many joined the faith because of Esther and Mordecai.

## Nehemiah the builder

A group of travellers, dusty and hanging their heads, arrived in Susa, Persia's capital. One of them spoke to the watchmen on the gate. "I have come from Jerusalem to see my brother, Nehemiah!" So they were led to the palace, for Nehemiah was cupbearer to King Artaxerxes himself, and was responsible for all the king's wine.

The travellers shared their news of Jerusalem with heavy hearts. "Those who have returned from exile are in deep distress. The city walls are still heaps of rubble – the people are defenceless and have lost hope!"

When Nehemiah heard the news, he wept for his home. For days, he fasted and prayed, and as the weeks passed his sadness grew. When Nehemiah waited on the king, his head was bent low with sadness, and his hand trembled.

"Are you ill? What's the matter?" the king asked. And Nehemiah told him about Jerusalem, praying under his breath as he did so.

The king respected Nehemiah. "Yes, you can go and make things right!" he said. "I will give you a cavalry escort, and letters of authority so you will have all you need."

As Nehemiah rode up to the city, he saw the people trying to grow food in the long-neglected fields. He saw the new Temple rising above heaps of rubble. How sad and poor it all looked. On his third night in the city, he got up, and rode through the deep shadows of the wall in secret. He saw that the walls and gates were in ruins.

"It's not good, is it?" he said to the city officials. "But we can rebuild it. God will be with us, and the king backs me in this work!"

"When do we start?" they replied. But Sanballat and Tobiah, two officials from the regions nearby, laughed at Nehemiah and schemed against the work.

The priests started building right away at the Sheep Gate, setting its heavy wooden doors in place. Groups worked on the wall near their homes, repairing the gates and gateways as they went. Sanballat and Tobiah were furious and sneered. "If a fox jumped on that wall, it would fall down!" they laughed. Then they threatened the builders. "We'll soon stop you!" they growled as they rattled their swords.

"Don't be afraid," said Nehemiah. "God is bigger than them! Work with a sword strapped to your sides, and listen out for a trumpet – the signal the wall is under attack." He stationed trumpeters and guards along the wall, and the people took turns to work from first light until the first stars. Half the people slept armed and dressed while the other half kept watch and built. And all the time the work went on, Sanballat and Tobiah sent messages saying, "You'll never finish!" and "Call that a wall? It's just a heap of stones!" But Nehemiah did not give up.

Then, after 52 days of work, the builders stretched their aching backs and smiled at the smooth, finished wall. And gradually, people returned to the rubble-filled city, and built houses out of the ruins.

Yet, still the people did not know how to live God's way. One day they all gathered in the city and asked the priest Ezra to teach them. He was a man of great learning, who had studied the Law of Moses deeply. He had returned to Jerusalem for this very task.

So Ezra brought out the scrolls, and looked at the great crowd before him: men and women, young and old. Then he began to read, praising God. By his side stood the Levites, the tribe who served in the Temple and studied the Law. As Ezra read out the Law in Hebrew, the ancient language of the Israelites, the Levites translated the words into Aramaic, a language of the Persian empire. For the people had forgotten Hebrew, the language of their ancestors. Now they spoke only Aramaic. The Levites explained the words fully as the two languages rose above the crowd. As they did so, the people realized they were not living as God wished, and they wept.

Nehemiah, Ezra, and the Levites said, "Don't be so downhearted. This is a great day. Have a feast, sharing with those who have little. For now we can do what is right! God's joy will be our strength." And the people made a promise to follow God's ways. Then singers and musicians with tambourines and harps processed along the wall, full of joy. The sound of their praises rolled over the countryside. Jerusalem became once more a beautiful city, whose people honoured God.

## God's promises

As the walls were rebuilt, so were the people. For God was building them into a new kind of kingdom. Isaiah the prophet wrote: "This is how to truly serve me: unbind people who are trapped by injustice, and lift up those who are ground down. Share your food with the hungry, and clothe the cold – that is how to live in light!"

The people listened to his words of bright hope. "There is much darkness in the world, but your light is coming! All nations will be drawn to you, and they, too, will shine."

People began to look for the Anointed One – a great leader who would bring healing like the warm rays of the rising sun. And the people treasured the words of Isaiah, who wrote of his coming:

*"A child is born to us,*
*a son is given.*
*Authority will rest*
*on his shoulders,*
*and his names will be*
*Wonderful Counsellor,*
*Mighty God,*
*Everlasting Father,*
*Prince of Peace.*
*His kingdom, his peace,*
*will roll across the lands,*
*and he will reign on the*
*throne of David for ever."*

# A New Beginning

Four hundred years had passed since the Jewish people came home from exile and settled once more in the land that had been promised them long ago. During that time other conquerors, other empires, had overcome them and taken control of their land – first the Greeks, and then the Romans. The Romans chose leaders for each region: Judea in the south, Galilee in the north, and Samaria in between.

The most powerful of these leaders was Herod the Great of Judea, named "King of the Jews" by the Roman emperor. He set to work transforming Jerusalem, rebuilding in the Roman style, in white stone and with many columns. The greatest of his works was a new Temple. One thousand priests had worked as stonemasons and carpenters to build this place of worship, the centre of Jewish life.

As well as priests who led worship in the Temple, there were also Pharisees who taught the people their faith. These teachers studied the scriptures – the Law – as well as the prophets and Jewish history, telling the people how they should live their lives. Through all this time, the Jewish people were still waiting for the Anointed One, the Messiah, who would come and lead them in God's way. Many believed he would be the one to set them free.

# The long silence is broken

Zechariah the priest paused in front of the altar, right by the curtain that screened the Holy of Holies from sight. He was close to the dark, silent heart of the Temple, where only the high priest ever went. This was the moment he had waited for through all his long years of service to God, and he looked around at the riches of the Temple in awe.

Then, he turned back to his task, and his hand shook as he placed the precious grains of incense in the burner. The grains glowed as he set the burner down on the altar, and fragrant smoke began to rise up into the high space above. He smiled. The offering had been made on behalf of all the Jewish people. His work was completed. He watched the white smoke for a while, then began to step back.

Suddenly, he gasped and stopped still. For standing at the right side of the altar was an angel of the Lord God. The old priest trembled, but the angel Gabriel spoke gently.

"Don't be afraid, Zechariah. I come to tell you that God has heard your prayers. You and your wife will be blessed with a child. Name him John. He will make you dance for joy – you and many others. He's going to be great. He will be filled with God's Spirit from his birth. And he will prepare the way for someone even greater."

This was wonderful news. For years Zechariah and his wife Elizabeth had prayed and longed for a child. It had been their brightest hope, but now childlessness was their sharpest pain.

"How can I believe that?" he answered, the words bitter in his mouth. "It's too late for us – now we're so old!"

"I bring you this message from the throne room of God! And still, you won't believe it? So that you know my words are trustworthy, you will not be able to speak until the day they come true."

Outside, the people who were waiting for Zechariah were whispering nervously. "Why is he taking so long? Could he have seen a vision, or heard God speak?" Then, at last, Zechariah staggered out, his eyes wide. He could not speak. He tried to gesture to them to tell them what had happened.

"Yes, he has seen a vision!" the others said.

So Zechariah returned to his home. Weeks drifted by in quietness, and Zechariah noticed his wife's eyes beginning to shine with delight. Elizabeth hid herself away, cherishing the secret of her pregnancy with careful joy. As she rested, Zechariah puzzled over Gabriel's words, and thought over the old prophecies that said these things must happen. His faith and hope began to grow again – the good news was only just beginning.

## Mary and the angel

Among the fields and vineyards of Nazareth, in Galilee, lived a girl named Mary. She was soon to be married to Joseph, a carpenter, who could trace his family back to David, the shepherd king.

Then, one day, astonishing news burst into Mary's quiet, hopeful life. The angel Gabriel came to her with a message.

"God is with you, Mary!" Mary gasped, and fell to her knees. "Don't be afraid. God smiles on you!" The angel spoke the astounding words gently, lovingly. "You will have a son and name him Jesus. He will be called great – the Son of the Most High God! The Lord God will give him the throne of his ancestor David, and his kingdom will never end!"

For a moment there was silence, as Gabriel's words filled the air – and Mary's mind. "But how can this be, as I am not yet married?" Mary asked.

"God's Holy Spirit will enfold you. Your child will be holy. Even Elizabeth, from your own family, is going to have a child, despite her age! She is now in her sixth month. So you see, nothing is impossible with God!"

Mary raised her eyes to Gabriel's face. "I am God's servant. Let it be as you say." And the angel left her alone, her mind spinning with the strange words.

Then Mary thought of Elizabeth. "The angel knew all about her – I must go to her." She got ready, and set off quickly for Elizabeth's home in Judea to the south, near Jerusalem.

As soon as she arrived at the house, she hurried to Elizabeth and took her hands. At the sound of Mary's voice, the baby leaped inside Elizabeth, and the Holy Spirit filled her. She understood at once what had happened to Mary.

"You are blessed among all women, and blessed is your unborn child!" she said. "Why have I been so honoured? Why should the mother of my Lord God come to visit me?" Elizabeth laughed, and put Mary's hand on her belly. "You see how my child leaps for joy at the sound of your voice?"

At last, Mary could say all that was on her heart.

*"I'm so full of joy my spirit is dancing*
*before God, my Lord, my Saviour.*
*God did not turn away from me*
*because I am poor, and now*
*I will be called blessed by*
*all the generations yet to come.*

*God, the great, the holy,*
*has done so much for me.*
*God brings down the powerful,*
*but lifts up the weak.*
*The well fed are empty,*
*and the table of the hungry*
*is piled high with good things.*

*"God looks at us with kindness,*
*giving hope to the hopeless,*
*caring for those who trust him,*
*remembering his promises to our people."*

So Mary stayed with Elizabeth for three long months, until it was time for Elizabeth's child to be born.

## The birth of John

News soon spread around the hills of Judea of how God had blessed Elizabeth and Zechariah with a child. On the day he was to be given a name, the house of the priest was filled with laughter, and tears of joy, as people gathered. They were going to call him Zechariah, after his father, as was the custom.

"No!" Elizabeth interrupted. "His name will be John."

The relatives and friends were taken aback, and turned to Zechariah. He signed for a writing tablet and wrote: "His name is John." Then his tongue was freed in his mouth, and immediately he began to speak. The long silence was broken at last.

He picked up his precious son and prophesied, speaking God's words.

*"God is so good! He is coming to save us,*
*through one of David's family!*
*And you, my own child,*
*will prepare the way.*
*The people will know*
*God's saving love, his forgiveness.*

*"God is sending us light like the rising sun*
*to shine on those lost in shadows,*
*and to guide us to the paths of peace."*

And as Zechariah's guests returned to their homes, full of what they had seen and heard, people began to hope again.

## *Joy to the world!*

The Roman emperor, Caesar Augustus, had ordered a census throughout the whole empire, when all the people would be counted, and taxed. The orders spread along straight Roman roads, and were proclaimed first in the white marble cities and ports, and then in the towns and villages of the countryside.

Even quiet Nazareth heard the news, and Mary and Joseph began to gather together their belongings, ready to travel to Bethlehem. That was Joseph's family home: he was descended from King David, of Bethlehem. They set off south on the crowded road, for the whole empire was travelling. But for Mary the journey was especially hard, and the road seemed never ending. It was nearly time for her baby to be born.

At last they came to Bethlehem, but it was not the end of their troubles. The town was noisy, bustling, and heaving with crowds, and Joseph searched anxiously for somewhere quiet for Mary to rest – her pains were beginning, and the baby would be born that night. The inn was already full of travellers, and the only place for them was a stable. There, among the animals, Mary gave birth to her firstborn son, wrapped him up tightly in swaddling clothes, and laid him in a manger full of hay. Then she rested next to the manger, smiling at the baby's tiny face.

There were shepherds who lived out on the hills nearby – the same hills where King David had once watched over the flocks, long ago. The sheep were sleeping in their fold under the shining stars, while the shepherds kept watch. Their fire flickered and crackled, and the lambs bleated sleepily for their mothers, but they were the only sounds. All was peaceful. All was well.

Suddenly, right there in the shepherds' simple camp, appeared an angel of the Lord, alight with God's glory and heaven's brightness. The shepherds gripped each other in terror, their skin prickling with fright.

"Don't be afraid, I'm bringing you good news – it will bring joy to all people!" The shepherds listened, awestruck, their faces glowing with the angel's light. "This is the day the good news begins, and this is the place. In the town of David, a saviour has been born. He is Christ, the Anointed One, the one you have been waiting for. And this is the sign that these words are true: you will find a baby wrapped tightly in swaddling clothes, lying in a manger."

The shepherds watched as light was added to light, voice to voice, until they were surrounded by a dazzling, heavenly host of angels, all praising God and saying:

*"Glory! Glory to God in the highest,*
*and on the earth be peace!"*

And then, in an instant, the angels were gone, and the shepherds were left in dark night shadows, listening to the sound of a distant wind. But their eyes still shone with heaven's light.

"Let's go and see for ourselves!" they called to one another as they raced over the dark, rocky fields to Bethlehem. There, they found Mary and Joseph, and, just as the angel had said, they found the baby wrapped tightly in swaddling clothes and lying in a manger. They saw him with their own eyes and spread the angel's message to all they met.

"The Promised One has come! The Christ, the Anointed One, has been born!"

The angel's words were on everyone's lips that night in Bethlehem. And, as the shepherds made their way back to their sheep, bursting with good news, Mary kept their words safe, like treasures, in her heart.

## The light of God has dawned

Mary and Joseph took the newborn Jesus to the Temple in Jerusalem, as God's Law required. They gave thanks for him with an offering of two doves. Now, in the city at that time were two people who had been waiting for the Anointed One. The first, Simeon, held on to God's promise that he would see the Messiah before he died. And on the very day that Mary and Joseph came, he was moved by the Holy Spirit to go to the Temple. He went straight up to them, took Jesus in his arms, and said, "Now I can leave this life in peace, for my eyes have seen God's plan to save all people. God has sent his light to everyone, even those far away from Israel. This light will shine on us and fill us with his glory." He spoke to Mary, too, of the pain that would pierce her own heart in years to come.

The second person was Anna, bent with age, but always worshipping, and always praying. The Temple was her home. As Simeon was speaking, she came up and praised God, knowing Jesus was the one they had all been waiting for, the one who would set them free.

## They followed a star

Far away from Jerusalem, in a land to the east, some wise men looked up at the clear night skies above the desert and saw a star rising. For years they had studied the movements of the stars and planets, and they had never seen anything like this before. They unrolled their charts and plotted its path.

"This means a new king has been born to the Jews!" they said to each other as they gave hurried orders to their servants to prepare for a journey.

When these strangely dressed foreigners arrived in Jerusalem, they began to ask, "Where is the one who has been born King of the Jews?" Troubled rumours spread through the city, for there had been no proclamation of any birth.

King Herod the Great's advisors approached him nervously.

"Your Majesty, strangers from the east have arrived in the city. They are searching for a child who they say has been born King of the Jews. They saw a sign in the heavens!" Herod caught his breath and turned white with fear. He had been given that title himself by the authority of Rome, building palaces and the great

Temple to spread his fame. What kind of king was coming to challenge him?

He asked his advisors, "Where is the Messiah, the Anointed One, to be born?" The scholars unrolled the scroll of the prophet Micah, and read out loud:

> *"Bethlehem will no longer be*
> *the least important of the towns.*
> *For from it will come a leader*
> *who will rule my people Israel*
> *like a shepherd king."*

"Bethlehem, eh?" murmured Herod. He gave orders for the wise men to be invited to the palace. He listened to their tale of the star with keen interest, nodding and smiling as if he were delighted at the news. He told them all about Bethlehem. "Go and find the child, then please send me a message so I can join you in your worship. What wonderful times these are!" Herod hid his crooked smile.

As the wise men set off from the cool marble and mosaics of the palace, they looked up at the sky once more. And there was the star, guiding them to Bethlehem. They followed, and found the child with his mother, Mary. She was astonished to receive such guests – who bowed low, and spoke of her son with reverence, and unwrapped precious gifts to lay at their feet.

She unclasped the caskets one by one. The first shone – it was full of gold. The second opened to a rich, sweet smell. "The smell of the Temple," Mary murmured to herself. It was frankincense, used in worship. The third contained an earthy, dark resin. It was myrrh, more valuable than gold, used in burials and for healing.

Mary looked up at her visitors, and thanked them for these extraordinary, extravagant gifts, as the smell of the incense and the myrrh hung in the air about them.

The wise men did not send word to Herod in Jerusalem, for that night they were troubled in their dreams about him. They paid attention to the warning, as they had to the star. So they slipped away, avoiding the town, to cross the desert once more.

## Escape to Egypt

Every day, Herod asked, "Well? Is there any message for me from Bethlehem?"

And every day, his attendants bowed as they answered. "No, Your Majesty, there is no message."

Herod's plan to be rid of this rival king was failing – and so another thought, chilling and terrible, began to circle in his mind.

Back in Bethlehem, God spoke to Joseph. An angel came to him in a dream.

"Get up now, Joseph! This minute! Take the child and his mother and run for Egypt. Herod is hunting for the child – he wants to kill him!"

And so, under cover of night, Mary and Joseph bundled their belongings together and slipped away from the town, carrying the sleeping child. They started out on their journey through the wilderness to Egypt.

After they left Bethlehem, great sorrow overtook the town. Herod's soldiers came and killed all the little boys under two years old. The mothers turned away from those who tried to comfort them, and wept bitterly for the loss of their children.

# My Father's house

After the death of Herod the Great, Joseph brought the family back to Nazareth, where they settled. Every year they travelled south to Jerusalem for the great festival of the Passover, when the Jewish people remembered how God had saved them from slavery in Egypt, and brought them to their own land, a land of plenty – the land where they now lived.

When Jesus was twelve years old, the family set out for Jerusalem's annual Passover celebrations with the excited crowds. Most of Nazareth had pulled their shutters closed and set off on the road together. The youngsters ran ahead, and back again, laughing and talking about their trip to the big city as they did every year. And Jerusalem's Temple was as busy, and as full of old friends, as they expected. The whole nation came together for this great remembering of their past, when they ate a lamb together, and flat bread, and drank wine, telling stories of how God had saved them and set them free.

All too soon it was time to go home, and the party from Nazareth was one of many pouring out of the city gates. At first, Mary and her husband were not worried when Jesus was not with them. But, as they asked after him, they soon realized that no one knew where he was. They hurried back to the city against the flow of the crowds, retracing every step they had taken. But he was nowhere to be found.

After three days of searching, they went to the Temple.

"Look!" said Mary, pointing across to Jesus, who was seated with the teachers of the Law, listening and asking questions. Everyone who heard him speak was amazed at his wisdom, but Mary hurried over at once through the crowd of listeners. "Why have you put us through this? We've been so worried about you!"

But Jesus replied, "Why did you have to look for me? Didn't you know I'd be here, in my Father's house?" Mary shook her head in confusion, but later, on the road home, she turned these words over in her mind, and treasured them in her heart.

So Jesus grew up in Nazareth, surrounded by the everyday life of the little town: the baking of bread, the making of wine, and the pressing of olives. He grew tall and wise, and those who knew of his birth were full of hope, waiting to see what this young man would become.

# Jesus the Teacher

*Prepare the way, make straight the paths*

An expectant murmur ran through the crowds who gathered in the hot, white sunlight. Some had walked through city streets, others through fields and vineyards, but all had come out into the desert of Judea to see one person.

It was John, son of Zechariah, who stood by the River Jordan.

John was no polished performer: he looked wild, dressed in rough clothes of camel hair held together by a leather belt. He was thin, eating only the locusts and wild honey he could find in the desert. But his words were full of power, full of life and holiness. He called out in a loud voice, "Repent! Turn your lives around and come back to God! His kingdom is near. Come and be washed clean!" And many came forward, full of sorrow for the wrongs they had done, and John baptized them in the River Jordan.

There were some, though, among the religious leaders who came and joined the crowds to look holy in front of everyone else – they thought they were good enough already and had no real need of change.

"You snakes!" John the Baptist spat. "We can tell what you are like by what you do – just as you can tell a tree by its fruit. You're not fooling anyone by this show of holiness!"

Most who came were not like that. They were truly hungry for a new beginning. For John taught them to hope. In his words, they caught a glimpse of something beyond their everyday lives. They understood that John the Baptist was preparing the way for something, or someone, astonishing.

"I baptize you with water, as a sign of your repentance: your turning back to God and his ways. But wait. There is one coming after me who is so much greater. I am not even worthy to carry his sandals for him. And when he comes, he will baptize you on the inside with the Holy Spirit and with fire. He will sort out the good from the bad, the wheat from the chaff!"

Then Jesus came down from Galilee in the north, and walked through the crowds toward John. John knew Jesus was the one they had been waiting for: the Messiah. Was Jesus really coming forward for baptism like everyone else?

"No!" said John, stepping back. "I need to be baptized by you – and yet you come to me – why?"

Jesus replied, "I must do everything that is right, and it is right to be baptized."

And so John agreed, and they stepped out into the flow of the Jordan. Jesus went down into the cool water, and was baptized.

As he came up, the bright sky broke open, and the Spirit of God came down gently and settled on him like a dove. A voice from heaven said, "This is my Son, the one I love, the one who brings me joy. I am very pleased with him."

## Alone for 40 days and 40 nights

Jesus, guided by the Holy Spirit, left the crowds and went deeper into the dry, hot desert. There, among the barren hills, Jesus spent 40 days and 40 nights without eating. He slept under the bright stars, and listened to the dry wind blowing through the valleys.

While hunger was still gnawing away at Jesus, the devil came to tempt him.

"If you really are the Son of God, you could order these stones to become warm, fresh bread."

But Jesus answered by quoting from God's Law: "People do not just live on bread. It is God's words that truly feed and satisfy."

The devil tried again, coaxing Jesus to throw himself off the Temple's highest point, to be saved by God's angels in front of all Jerusalem. Once again, Jesus quoted the scriptures: "Do not put God to the test."

The third time, the devil showed him all the kingdoms of the world, rich and magnificent. "It's all yours if you'll worship me!" he said.

"Get away from me!" replied Jesus. "It is written in the Law: 'Worship only God – worship him with your whole heart!' " Then the devil left him, and angels came to care for him.

## The fishermen

Jesus travelled back to Galilee and left his home town of Nazareth to settle in Capernaum, by the side of the lake. He began to preach, saying, "Turn your lives around, for God's kingdom is very near!" His words carried over the water to the fishermen on their boats, who stopped their work to listen.

One day, Jesus strolled by the lapping water, watching the net makers, the fishermen, and the boat builders at work. There, he saw two brothers throwing their nets out over the water. They were Simon and Andrew.

Jesus called out to them, "Come with me – follow me. There are bigger fish than these for you to catch. You'll be fishers of people!"

Their faces broke into broad grins, and they hurried to bring the boat back to shore. They left their nets and joined Jesus, walking with him along the shore. They stopped where Zebedee's boat was tied up in the shallows. James and John, Zebedee's sons, were mending the tears in their nets. Jesus called to them, and they jumped into the cool water and splashed their way over to him. They became his followers, his disciples.

## Water into wine

On the third day after Jesus called his disciples, Jesus went with them to a wedding in Cana, near Lake Galilee. The whole community was there, eating and drinking, dancing and laughing, blessing the young man and woman who were starting their life together. But Jesus' mother, Mary, noticed that the wine had run out and said to her son, "They have no more wine!"

"Dear mother, why are you telling me this? Now is not my time."

But, later, Jesus spoke to the servants. "Fill those jars with water!" he said. For there were six large stone water jars nearby – the sort that were used to store the pure, fresh water the Jewish people used to cleanse and purify themselves before worship. The servants filled the jars with water and, puzzled, dipped their serving jugs into the newly filled jars. They poured some out for the host, as Jesus had told them.

Then the host called the bridegroom over, a broad smile on his face. "By now people are usually serving the rough wine – but this wine is really good – wonderful! You've kept the best until last." He gulped another warm mouthful of the wine that had been water as the servants served the wedding guests.

Jesus had taken the water from the stone jars and turned it into fine wine. When his disciples saw what had happened, and saw the servants pouring out new wine for all the guests at the wedding, they gasped in wonder. They had caught a glimpse of Jesus' glory, and the glory of God's kingdom. The disciples put their faith in the one who turned water into wine.

## Good news in Galilee

Jesus went around the whole of Galilee, teaching in the synagogues, where the Jews gathered to worship. He told people that God, who is loving and just, was among them, building heaven on earth. And he showed God's love by healing those who were sick. In this way, news about him travelled through the land, and many were drawn toward him. Those whose lives were twisted with pain, those who could not move, those who were haunted and troubled by evil, all these and more were brought to him. People came from nearby fields and villages, and from many miles away, and followed Jesus with eager hope.

## The sabbath in Capernaum

It was the sabbath, a day for the Jewish people to remember God's gift of rest to them since the beginning of the world. It was a holy time in which to lay aside back-breaking work, but it had become snared and snagged in a knot of rules and regulations. This sabbath, Jesus spoke at Capernaum's synagogue. When he talked, the murmuring at the back stopped, and all turned eagerly to hear. He did not teach like the experts in God's Law, picking at details, but as one who truly understood, shining clear bright light into the ways of God. But there was one person there whose life was full of darkness, troubled by an evil spirit.

"What do you want, Jesus of Nazareth – to destroy us? I know you… You're the Holy One – the one sent by God!"

"Be quiet!" cut in Jesus, and the voice stopped. "Leave him alone!" he ordered, and the troubled man shook, and then was still.

First, there was silence as all looked at the now calm, smiling figure; then the people turned to each other and said, "This is new teaching – it has power over evil! At last, here's something real!" The people went home, talking of all they had seen and heard.

Jesus, James, and John went to Simon and Andrew's house, where Simon's mother-in-law was lying ill. "Will you see her?" Simon asked quietly, and Jesus drew close to her bed. She was feverish under a thin blanket, her hair stuck to her burning forehead. Jesus took her hot hand, and coolness washed through her. Jesus helped her up; she smiled to see guests in the house, and straightaway she began to look after them.

As the sky glowed softly with the setting sun, and the sabbath drew to a close, people began to gather at the door of the house, bringing with them those who suffered. Jesus healed many, and drove out evil spirits, silencing them – for they knew who he really was. The warm evening air was full of the laughter of the healed, and the dancing joy of those who loved them.

At dawn the next day, Simon and the others got up. "Where is he?" they asked, looking at the empty place where Jesus had slept. They went out searching, and eventually found him far from the town, in a solitary place. For he had been spending the quiet dawn hours in prayer. "Everyone is looking for you!" they said.

But Jesus replied strangely. "Let's go somewhere else. There are other villages nearby. I must take the good news there, too. For that is why I have come."

## The calling of Levi

Jesus was walking by Lake Galilee once more, followed by hopeful crowds. As he walked, he talked with the people who came with him. Then he stopped by a little stall among those clustered on the shoreline. It was not the most popular place in the market, for it was the place where Levi, a Jew, sat to collect the taxes for the Romans, the occupiers who ruled over them. Tax collectors were hated as traitors and despised as cheats. So when Jesus stopped, the crowds looked on expectantly, wondering what Jesus would say.

As Jesus' eyes met Levi's, the tax collector rose slowly to his feet. Jesus stretched out his hand. "Come and join us! Come, follow me!" Levi's face lit up with joy as he walked alongside Jesus. A little nervously, he invited the teacher for dinner.

It was quite a party at Levi's house. Jesus came with his disciples, and Levi's friends soon joined them. They were a lively group of tax collectors and other people who were known to break the Jewish laws. They listened to Jesus, for many had become his followers. How shocked the teachers of the Law were when they heard that a rabbi like them was keeping company with such people! They asked his disciples, "Why does your rabbi eat with tax collectors and wrongdoers?"

When he heard about this questioning, Jesus replied, "The strong and fit don't go to the doctor, sick people do! This is what I have come for: to call people who have gone wrong in their lives to something new, something better."

# Disputes and healing

Many people were puzzled by Jesus' teaching, and how he lived. They asked him, "The Pharisees and their disciples, and John the Baptist's disciples, all fast. Yours don't – why?"

Jesus replied, "Do the guests at a wedding go without food while the bridegroom is with them? No – but later, when he leaves, they will fast." And he went on to explain how his new teaching needed new ways of living.

"No one sews a new patch of material on old, torn clothes. The new patch will shrink and pull away from the old cloth, making the tear worse. A new patch needs to go on new clothes. And no one pours new wine into an old leather bottle. The new wine will burst the old, brittle wineskin. Instead, new wine needs a new, supple wineskin."

One sabbath, Jesus was walking through fields of golden, blowing corn, with his disciples at his side. As they walked, they plucked some of the corn, and rubbed the papery husks off in the palms of their hands. For this, too, Jesus was questioned by the Pharisees. It seemed to them that what Jesus and his disciples did was harvesting – working. And work was forbidden on the sabbath day of rest.

"Don't you remember reading about what King David did when he was hungry?" Jesus asked them. "He ate some of the holy bread from the Temple, which only the priests were allowed to eat. The sabbath is made for people, not people for the sabbath. The sabbath is there to bless us!" So Jesus was watched carefully, to see if he would break the rules that were so important to the Pharisees.

They did not have long to wait. For one sabbath, at the synagogue, Jesus saw a man whose hand was damaged, shrivelled and lying useless on his lap. He knew the people were asking themselves, "Will he heal on the sabbath – isn't that work, and forbidden?"

So Jesus asked the man to stand up in front of everyone. He turned and looked at the faces of the Pharisees, set as hard as stone, and said, "Tell me – what does God's Law say we should do on the sabbath – good or evil? Should we save, or should we kill?"

The Pharisees, who saw themselves as experts in God's Law, looked at the man with their cold eyes, but they gave no answer. How that grieved Jesus. "Stretch out your hand!" he said. As the man began to try to lift his hand, he felt it growing firm and strong. The man turned his hand over, flexed his fingers, and his face shone with sudden joy. He was free! Now he could work to feed his family, he could cradle his children.

But the Pharisees did not see this. They only saw that they had been challenged, and had lost, and they began to scheme against one whose authority was so much greater than theirs.

## The choosing of the Twelve

Wherever Jesus went, he was buffeted by crowds longing for healing, for a touch from him. He went up the steep rocky slopes of a mountain, taking just twelve from the crowds with him. These were the ones that would be closest to him and learn from him so that they, too, could preach and drive out evil in his name. The Twelve were: Simon (also known as Peter); James and John; Andrew, Philip, Bartholomew, Matthew, Thomas, James son of Alphaeus, Thaddaeus, Simon the Zealot, and Judas Iscariot.

# The sower

Jesus and the Twelve travelled from village to village, telling people the good news of God's kingdom. This kingdom was so different from the one the people knew: the cold power of white-marbled Rome. As they went, they were joined by others who had been healed or set free from evil by Jesus – Mary Magdalene, Joanna, Susanna, and many more. They gave generously from their wealth to support the band of disciples, which was growing as quickly as new vine shoots in spring.

Once, when Jesus was surrounded by a crowd of eager listeners, he told them this story.

"One dry, bright day, when the wind was still, a farmer went out to sow seed. He took handfuls of grain from the flat basket he carried and, with a flick of the wrist, scattered seed, hopeful for its growth. But some of the seed fell on the path, where the passing of many feet trampled it, and the birds swooped down and ate it. Some fell on dry rock. After the soft rains, it swelled and sprouted. But then it withered, for its roots could find no water. Some landed among the thorns, which grew so fast that they soon smothered the tender new shoots. But some landed on good soil, where it grew up, and ripened. When the time was right, the farmer came back and harvested a crop from it, a hundred times more than was sown."

After the crowds had gone, and Jesus was left with the disciples, they asked him, "What does that story mean?" And Jesus answered:

"The seed is the word – God's word. The seed that fell on the path is like the seed that falls in some hearts – it's snatched away by the devil before it takes root, before those people begin to believe. The seed that falls on the rocks is seed that falls where there is little depth – at first, God's words bring joy to those people, but there are no roots, and when trouble comes their faith withers away. The thorny places are like hearts choked up with worry, with riches and pleasures. There's no space for God's word to grow. But some seed does fall on good soil – the word takes root in hearts that are ready, and they hold on to it. In time, the word gives a rich crop in people's lives, and they are fruitful."

## Living God's way

The crowds followed Jesus wherever he went. He was a healer, and teacher, and bringer of hope for many whose lives were scarred with hardship and pain. He went and sat on the mountain side, and his followers came to learn from him. He began by teaching them about happiness.

*"You are blessed when you know how poor you are inside,*
*for then you are open to God and his ways.*
*You are blessed when you are sad,*
*for then you will feel a loving hand on your shoulder.*
*You are blessed when you are gentle and humble;*
*you will see all of earth's good things, there for you.*
*You are blessed when you hunger for what is right;*
*you will be satisfied.*
*You are blessed when you live generously and kindly,*
*for you will be treated with kindness, too.*
*You are blessed when you are wholeheartedly good;*
*nothing will stand between you and God.*

*You are blessed when you work for peace;*
*you will be called one of God's children.*

"You are blessed when hard times come because of your faith in me, for they persecuted the prophets of the past, too; you will have a great reward in heaven.

"You are salt and light in this world. Salt gives taste to everything. And light shines so all can see. You don't hide it away! This is what you should be like, making things better for all."

"Do you think I've come to do away with the scriptures – God's Law and the teachings of the prophets? Well, you're wrong. I haven't come to throw out the Law, but to show you the great, lasting truth of it – how to really live God's way.

"You all know that the Law tells you not to kill, but what about those spiteful words you say that cut to the heart? Saying them puts your spirit in danger. So, if you are praying, and remember that you've hurt someone, go and make peace with them first and then come back to God. Don't let quarrels lie smouldering. Do all you can to make things right.

"The same goes for all the other laws. Some are to stop you doing wrong things, like breaking your promises, or wanting what isn't yours. And others are to encourage you to do what is right, like praying, or giving to the needy. You could keep the laws strictly, and look like you were doing the right thing, while inside your thoughts were wrong and twisted. God's way is to get rid of the bad inside you. Then you'll grow strong, like a healthy tree that gives sweet, healthy fruit."

"You all know what the Law says about getting your own back – 'An eye for an eye, and a tooth for a tooth' – but this is what I say: Don't fight back against an evil person. If they hit you on one cheek, turn and offer them the other. If someone wants to take what's yours, give it to them, and give something extra too. If they force you to do something for them, why not do more than they ask?

"You have heard 'Love your neighbour and hate your enemy', but this is what I say: Love your enemy and pray for those who hurt you. Think about it. God sends sunshine and blessings to everyone – whatever they're like. This is the Father's nature, generous and open-handed. If you want to be a child of God, you need to take after God.

"It's all too easy to see what other people are doing wrong – to find fault. Remember, the harsh standards you use to judge others will be used on you. Why do you look at the speck in your brother's eye when there's a great plank in your own? Sort yourself out first, then you might see clearly enough to help.

"So always think about how you would like to be treated, and treat other people with the same kindness. That's what the Law and prophets are really saying."

"Don't give all your life to hoarding things. Rust and moths can ruin them, and thieves can take them from you. Things don't last. But there is a treasure that will – God's treasure. Keep that in heaven's storeroom and you will know it's safe! No thief can get to it there, and nothing can spoil it. Wherever your treasure is, that's where your heart will always be.

"Don't worry, then, about what to eat and what to wear. Life is more important than food, and the body more precious than clothes. Watch these birds, fed by God. They don't cram barns with food, yet they have enough. Look at the bright flowers nodding in the breeze. Not even King Solomon wore robes as colourful as those wild flowers. God feeds the birds and clothes the hillsides with beauty, so trust God to care for you, too. Live God's way, look to God's kingdom, and God will give you all these things. So don't worry about tomorrow."

"Ask, and it will be given to you. Look, and then you will find. And if you knock, the door will open. Everyone who asks receives, everyone who looks finds, and everyone who knocks will see the door opening for them. When your children ask you for bread, do you give them stones? Or if they ask for fish, do you give them snakes? Of course not! You know how to give good things to your children. God is your heavenly Father, giving good things to all who ask.

"But what you get depends on what you really want. Some pray standing in the synagogues, where people gather to worship. Some pray in the streets for all to see. They want people to look up to them, so they've already got what they wanted. When you pray, it's for God alone. Do it privately, not for show. And don't think you have to use long words and fine phrases. God knows what is in your heart, so just talk to God. Pray like this:

> *"Our Father in heaven,*
> *hallowed be your name,*
> *your kingdom come,*
> *your will be done on earth as in heaven.*
> *Give us today our daily bread.*
> *Forgive us our sins,*

*as we forgive those who sin against us.*
*Lead us not into temptation,*
*but deliver us from evil."*

"You have listened to my words," Jesus said to the people gathered around him. "But will you put them into practice? Will they become part of your life?" He paused, and then told a story.

"If you take these words into your hearts and lives, you are like a wise builder. The wise builder found a high, solid rock, and built his house on that. It was firm and strong. Nothing shook it. Not even the sudden storm that came one day. It turned the streams into brown torrents of water, and beat angrily against the walls and shutters. All outside was raging flood and pouring rain. But inside the builder was safe, firm on the rock.

"But if you hear my words and go away, and nothing changes in your life, you are like a foolish builder. He chose a sandy spot for his home and all was well, as long as the sun shone. But when the black clouds gathered over this house, it was a different story. As the rain poured down and the streams swelled, the sand began to shift, twisting the wind-battered walls. The house could not stand. It fell down with a crash."

This teaching was so fresh, so new, so full of power, that the people sat listening to Jesus in amazement.

## The rich young man

A young man came up to Jesus and sat down by him, smoothing out his linen clothes.

"Teacher," he asked, "what good thing must I do to have eternal life?"

"Why ask about 'good'? There's only One who is truly good. If you want eternal life, obey God's commands," Jesus answered.

"Which ones?" asked the young man, for there were many.

"Don't murder or steal, don't lie, be faithful, honour your parents, and love your neighbour as yourself."

"Yes, I've kept all those – so what's missing?"

"If it's perfection you're after, go and sell everything you have. Give everything to the poor, then you'll have treasure in heaven. And come, follow me!" Jesus smiled, but the young man stood up, shocked, and turned to leave, with his head bowed low. His great riches pulled him away.

Jesus said to his disciples, "It's hard for the rich to enter God's kingdom. It's easier for a camel to slip through the eye of a needle than for a rich man to enter God's kingdom."

The disciples were amazed – surely riches were a sign of God's blessing. "Then what hope is there for anyone?" they asked.

"None if you think you can get to God by your own efforts, but every hope if you trust in God! Many who think they are first will be at the end of the queue, and the last will be first."

## The greatest

"Who is the greatest in the kingdom of heaven?" the disciples asked Jesus, sure that they would be mentioned in the answer. But Jesus called a little child to stand among them.

"Now listen, this really matters!" he said. "You must become like a little child to enter the kingdom. If you stop thinking about your own importance, and go back to being like this child, you'll be great in God's kingdom.

"You need to give children the welcome you would give a guest;

in doing so, you're welcoming me. If anyone harms a little child, or leads them into wrongdoing, it would be better for that person to have a huge millstone tied around their neck and be thrown into the sea. Don't look down on the little children. God loves and protects them, keeping a careful watch over them, for their angels in heaven always see my Father's face."

## Lost sheep

Jesus smiled at the little child standing in front of him, and at the crowds of children playing nearby, and told this story.

"A farmer owns a hundred sheep, and one of them wanders away. She gets lost. What will the farmer do? He'll leave the 99 grazing peacefully on the hillside, and go off to search for the missing one. He'll look for her in bushes and behind rocks, and he'll keep on looking until he finds his lost sheep. Then he'll pick her up, put her over his shoulders, and carry her safely home. He'll be very happy to have found the one lost sheep.

"It's the same with the Father in heaven. He doesn't want any of these little ones to be lost."

When people crowded around Jesus with their children, the disciples tried to send them away; but Jesus prayed for the children, and put his hands on them to bless them. He said, "Let the little children come to me. Do nothing to stop them. Remember, the kingdom of heaven belongs to people who are like these children."

## Nicodemus the Pharisee

One night, Nicodemus slipped through the dark streets of Jerusalem to visit Jesus, who was staying in the city. He came alone, not wanting to be seen. Nicodemus was an important man: a well-known Pharisee, and a leader of the Jewish people. Many of the Pharisees did not approve of Jesus.

Nicodemus came to the house where Jesus was staying, and went in. He stepped into a room lit by a small lamp that threw a warm circle of light into the shadows. And there was Jesus, sitting in the lamplight, ready to welcome him in. Nicodemus joined Jesus and began to speak the words that were running through his mind.

"Rabbi, we know you are a teacher who has come from God. The miracles you do prove that!"

As Nicodemus spoke, Jesus looked into his face, searching his eyes by the warm light. He knew this man was wise, so when Jesus broke the silence, he spoke to Nicodemus of the deep truths of God's ways.

Nicodemus listened as Jesus spoke of God's Spirit: how it could not be seen, but could be felt, as the wind is felt when it blows. Jesus spoke too of a new type of birth: a birth of the Spirit, so that all people could see God's kingdom with the fresh eyes of a child.

Then, Jesus spoke of how much God loved the world: enough to send his only son to die, so that everyone who believes in him could have a new life that would last for ever, a life full of light and truth.

Nicodemus listened, opening his mind to take in these extraordinary words. And as Nicodemus stepped out of the circle of lamplight, and walked home through the shadowy streets, he turned Jesus' words over in his mind, beginning to understand.

# Living water

It was hot when the woman went to get water from the well, near her home town of Sychar in Samaria. As she drew near, she saw a Jewish man sitting there, in the shade. She hesitated a moment, nervous of this stranger. For the Jews and Samaritans had been enemies for centuries, since the time when God's people went into exile. "But," she thought, "I must have water," and she carried on walking to the well.

The man was Jesus. He had left Jerusalem and was making his way back to Galilee. His disciples were buying food, leaving him to rest from the burning sun. He looked up at the woman.

"Will you give me a drink?" he asked, with a thirsty smile. Jews and Samaritans never ate or drank together: it was against all the laws and customs.

"You, a Jew, are asking me, a Samaritan, for a drink?" She was so startled she nearly dropped her water jug.

"If you knew who I was, you'd ask me, and I would give you real, life-giving water!"

"How can you get water? You have nothing to hold it in!"

"If you drink from the well, you'll be thirsty again. If you drink the water I offer, it will become like a clear spring within you, bubbling over with eternal life!"

"Sir, I would like that water!" she replied. But Jesus questioned her about how she lived, and amazed her by revealing her secrets: things she had kept hidden, for shame. Could this man be a prophet?

She ran back to town, telling everyone. They invited Jesus and the disciples to stay, and he taught them for two days.

The people of the town said to the woman, "Now, we don't

just believe in Jesus because of what you said. We've heard the truth for ourselves!"

## Going alone

Jesus went from town to town, from village to village, telling everyone the good news of God's kingdom. Wherever he went, he healed and gave hope. As he turned to face the huge, needy crowd following him, he saw how lost they were. They were like sheep wandering in a rocky land, with no shepherd to guide them to good grazing.

He said to his disciples, "Look, these people are like fields of corn waiting for the harvest. Pray for more workers. Pray that this good harvest will be gathered in."

And so Jesus called the Twelve to him, and taught them how to gather in the harvest of people. He gave them authority to do what he had been doing – to drive out evil, and to heal all kinds of sickness.

"Go to the lost sheep of Israel. Find them and bring them back. You have been so blessed, now it's your turn to give. Heal, raise the dead, cure the sick, drive out evil. Don't take any money with you. Do good, and you'll earn your keep. Find people of peace, and stay with them.

"Not everyone will welcome you, though. You'll be whipped in the synagogues, put on trial before governors and kings, before the Romans. Don't worry. God will give you the right words to say. My message of God's love will divide people. You will need to be ready to face any trial to follow me. It will not be easy. But all who receive you will receive me, and in this way God's blessing will spread."

# John's question

John the Baptist had been shut away in prison for speaking out against the local king. He sent some of his disciples to his cousin, Jesus.

"Are you the one John was expecting, or should we look for someone else?" they asked. The crowd fell silent. John's preaching had been so full of fire. Could he now be doubting?

"Go back and tell John what you see and hear. The blind can see, the lame can walk, the sick are healed, the deaf can hear, and the good news is preached to the poor." John's disciples knew these words. They were part of Isaiah's prophecy about the coming Messiah. The answer was clear.

As they were leaving, Jesus turned to the murmuring crowds. "What did you go out into the desert to see – someone changeable and doubting, blown this way and that like a reed bending in the wind? A man in elegant clothes? No, you went to see a prophet. And you were right, for John is a truly great prophet. From the day John began to preach, the kingdom of God has been marching forward with great power."

# God's Kingdom — Signs and Stories

## *The faith of a Roman*

The centurion stood with his hands behind his back, watching his most loyal servant's dry lips as they moved without sound.

"That's enough!" he said to those who were trying to coax the servant to drink, and they slipped back, away from the couch. For a moment the centurion leaned down, his ear close to the man's mouth, but his breath was growing fainter. He was near death. The centurion strode out to the courtyard and looked up at the road. He saw Jesus in the distance, with his followers behind. Quickly, he spoke to the Jewish elders who stood by the gate, and they turned and walked toward Jesus.

"Rabbi," they said, "we come to see you at the request of the Roman centurion stationed here." The crowds watched Jesus carefully – what would he do? For the Roman soldiers were an occupying force. They were the enemy. "As you know, this centurion has treated us kindly, paying for our synagogue. Now his servant is very ill, and he asks for you to heal him."

Jesus did not hesitate. He quickened his pace into Capernaum. As he came close to the army garrison, the centurion's friend came out with a message. "Sir, the centurion sends you this message: 'Please don't trouble to come into my home. Just say the word, and my servant will be well. I'm a man of authority. I give orders, and they are obeyed. I know you, too, are a man of authority – at your command, the illness will leave.' "

Jesus stopped, and turned around to those following. "Do you hear that?" he asked. "I haven't found such faith in all of Israel!"

Then, as the friend returned to the garrison, they all heard shouts of joy and laughter. For the servant had been healed.

## Grief to joy

Soon after this, Jesus moved on to the town of Nain. He was followed closely by the crowds, and by his disciples. As they were drawing near to the town gates they saw a sad procession coming out, on their way to the burial place. A young man had died: the only child of his mother, who was a widow. She had lost all she had loved most, and followed the procession weeping, leaning on her friends.

Jesus' heart was filled with compassion when he saw her. "Don't cry!" he said.

Then he touched the open coffin, and those carrying it stood still. Jesus spoke. "Young man, get up!"

And he sat up, and began to speak. Jesus took his hand, now warm, and placed it in his mother's tight grasp.

All the townspeople gasped, awestruck, and said, "A great prophet is among us," and "God has come to help his people!" People talked of this miracle as they travelled along the roads, and word of it spread through fields, vineyards, and olive groves all over Galilee and Judea.

# Through the roof

When the people of Capernaum learned that Jesus had come back home to them, they left their ploughs and cooking pots and rushed to see him. They filled the house, and others crowded outside and peered through the doors and windows. There, they listened to every word he spoke.

Then, suddenly, they heard a scratching and pounding, as if someone was trying to dig down through the roof, and those inside the house jumped back as dust and clay began to fall down. Soon, a shaft of sunlight broke through from the bright sky onto the dark floor by Jesus' feet, and a man on a mat was lowered down on ropes, cloaked in swirls of dust caught in the light. Jesus looked up at the hole in the ceiling, and at the faces of four friends who peered down into the shadows.

"We couldn't get in, and our friend needs help – he's paralysed, can't move!" they said.

Jesus warmed to their faith and, smiling, said to the man on the mat, "Your sins are forgiven!"

A murmur spread through the crowd. "What did he say?" everyone asked.

But the teachers of the Law were grinding their teeth. "How dare he!" they thought. "No one can forgive sins except God. This is an outrage against God, a blasphemy!"

Jesus answered their thoughts. "What's easiest – to say 'Your sins are forgiven' or 'Get up, and walk'? But to show you I do have authority to forgive…" Here, he got down low next to the man, and said in a quiet voice, "Get up, pick up your mat, and walk home!"

And so he did – laughing and leaping over the heads of those sitting jammed together in the house, squeezing through the doorway and bounding out into the dazzling sunlight. How joyfully his friends cheered as they leaped down from the roof after him! The good news grew and spread.

## Small seeds

As Jesus sat in a boat close to the shore, he taught those who had gathered in the fields by the side of the lake. He explained God's ways.

"This is what God's kingdom is like," he began. "A man scatters seed on the soil. And the seed grows, whether he sleeps or wakes. He doesn't know why or how it happens. All by itself the corn comes up through the soil, and in time the man returns, and gathers in a good harvest."

He told a second story. "How shall I tell you about God's kingdom? It's like a man who digs down in the earth and plants a tiny mustard seed – it's so small that a puff of wind could take it out of the palm of his hand. Yet it grows and spreads into the largest plant in the garden, with branches where the birds can come and shelter."

## Storm!

"Let's go now, over to the other side of the lake!" Jesus said to his fishermen-disciples. So they checked the sails and tightened the ropes, making sure all was ready. Then, as the boat pulled away from shore, Jesus lay down, and fell asleep to the gentle lull of the waves. But soon, the water began to swell, and the rocking grew urgent, worrying, as water slopped into the little boat.

Then the fishermen looked up and saw darkness overshadowing

the lake, as a sudden, powerful wind funnelled down through the hills, tearing at the deep water, sending waves crashing into the creaking, groaning boat. The disciples hauled in the sails, and tried to steer through the towering, black water, but it was no good. These fishermen knew they were in trouble.

They lurched unsteadily to Jesus, and woke him. "Lord, save us, we're going to drown!" they shouted above the roar of the wind.

Jesus rose to his feet and turned to face the storm. "Wind, stop! Waves, be still!" And the wind stopped with a gasp, and waves flattened to smooth silver, and the disciples were filled with quiet awe. "Why were you so afraid? Where is your faith?" Jesus asked them.

"Who is this?" they whispered to each other. "Even the wind and waves obey him!"

## Jairus and his daughter

The crowd stood on the Galilean shores of the lake, waiting for Jesus to return. They watched the little fishing boat grow larger and larger, its sail full and billowing before the wind. They crowded around as Jesus landed, but then a murmur spread among them as a man came forward.

"It's Jairus, come to see Jesus. Have you heard? His little girl is very ill." Jairus was the head of their synagogue. They stepped aside to let him through, and watched as he fell on his knees before Jesus.

"My daughter is dying, Master," he sobbed. "She's so young, only twelve years old. Please come to her and heal her." Jesus bent down and grasped his hand, helping him to his feet.

They made their way quickly toward Jairus's home through

the jostling crowds. Among the crowds was a woman. "If I can just touch the edge of his prayer shawl, I will be healed!" she murmured to herself. And she reached out her hand.

"Who touched me?" asked Jesus, turning on his heels. Everyone stepped back. Peter said, "Master, look at the crowds! We've all been nudging and jostling you!"

"Someone touched me. I felt power flow from me." The woman pulled her scarf down over her face, took one quiet step forward, and sank to the ground at Jesus' feet. She spoke out about the bleeding that she had suffered from for years, and how no one had been able to help her. Then she looked up, her scarf slipping back.

"But you healed me, Master!" she said, and smiled.

"Go in peace now, my daughter. Your faith has brought you healing."

But even at this moment, someone from Jairus's household came to him. "Your daughter has taken her last breath. Come home and leave the Teacher. It's too late."

Jesus turned to Jairus and said, "Don't be afraid. Believe, and she will be healed." And they carried on walking, followed by the crowds.

When Jesus got to the door, he stopped. "Just Peter, John, and James," Jesus said. "Everyone else must stay out here." And so those three, and the girl's father and mother, went to the little girl, following Jesus. They found her lying white and silent, while all around the black-cloaked figures of the mourners were gathering. Jesus sent them to wait outside, too. "There's no need for tears," he said. "She's just sleeping!"

The mourners sneered as they went past. They knew death when they saw it. But Jesus took the girl's still hand and held it.

"Little girl, get up!" he said to her gently, and her life returned to her in a shudder of breath. She stretched, and stood up, smiling as brightly as the sunshine. Her parents gasped, stunned.

"She'll be hungry!" Jesus said, and they bustled away to bring her favourite food. He also told them not to tell anyone what had happened.

## Seeing what the Father does

One sabbath, Jesus was in Jerusalem. He came to the pool of Bethesda, which means "House of Mercy". The pool, with its steep steps, was surrounded by covered colonnades. Under their shade lay many who were sick, waiting to enter the water when it welled up, for they believed that the water could heal them. Jesus went and sat down by one man, and asked him, "Do you want to be healed?"

"Sir, there's no one to help me down into the pool. I've been an invalid for 38 years. How can I reach the water?"

So Jesus said, "Just get up! Take your mat and walk away!" – and he did so.

Some teachers of the Law stopped him. "What do you think you're doing, carrying a mat on the sabbath? Don't you know that's work, and forbidden?" And the man told them what had happened. How angry they were at Jesus – a sabbath-breaker, they called him.

"My Father is always at work, so I, too, am working!" Jesus said. The teachers of the Law gasped, shocked. He was talking as if he were God's equal!

"I don't do anything by myself," Jesus went on. "I see what my Father is doing and do the same!"

# Bread in the wilderness

Some time later, near the Passover, Jesus and his disciples sailed to the far side of Lake Galilee; a huge crowd followed them eagerly, for they had seen Jesus heal the sick.

Jesus and his disciples arrived first and sat down on the mountain side. From there, they could see the dusty crowds draw nearer.

Jesus turned to Philip. "Where shall we buy bread for them to eat?"

Philip frowned. "It would take eight months' wages to buy enough bread – and that would be less than a mouthful each!"

But Andrew, Simon's brother, spoke up. "Look, there's a boy here with five barley loaves and two small fish…" The other disciples stared in astonishment. "But that won't go far among so many!" he added quickly.

Jesus smiled. "Tell the people to sit down!"

The people sat down on the soft green grass, glad to rest after their long walk. Then the boy handed his food over to Jesus, and sat down too, not taking his eyes off his loaves and fish. Jesus lifted up the bread, and gave thanks for it, breaking it in his hands. The disciples passed the broken bread among the crowds. And then, Jesus blessed the fish in the same way, and the fish, too, were passed among the crowds.

It took time to share the food, for there were about 5,000 people sitting by the shore. A hush fell over the crowd as they realized that everyone, from the little boy to the oldest person, had enough to eat.

"Don't let any go to waste – collect up the leftovers!" Jesus said. And they collected twelve basketfuls. The crowds remembered the twelve tribes of Israel; perhaps Jesus could feed their whole nation? They remembered, too, how Moses gave bread to the people of Israel in the wilderness. Could Jesus be even greater than Moses?

"Let's make him king!" the crowds shouted, marching forward. But Jesus slipped away into the mountains, alone.

In time, his disciples found him. "Why do you come for me?" he asked them. "Did you really understand this sign of God's ways, or do you come because you ate your fill?" He continued, "God's bread from heaven gives life to all the world. And I am the bread of life. Come to me, and you will never be hungry again."

## Blind

The blind man sat by the side of the road, his begging bowl in his lap, listening to the voices and footsteps that came and went, hour after hour. Suddenly, one group stopped, and the blind man heard them talking – talking about him.

"Jesus," he heard one say, "did this man sin, or was it his parents who did wrong? Why was he born blind?"

"It's got nothing to do with who did what, or who is to blame!" the one they called Jesus answered. "He is blind so that God's glory can be seen in his life. And as long as there is light, I must do God's work. While I am here, I am the light of the world." There was murmuring at this strange answer. But the blind man sat still and quiet, waiting.

"I'm going to put some mud on your eyes," said a calm voice close to his ear – Jesus' voice. And as he spoke, the man felt thick mud smeared on his sightless eyes.

The voice spoke again. "Go now – I am sending you to wash in the Pool of Siloam, 'the pool of the sent'!" The man felt his way to the pool, and washed. How cool it was. Then he blinked away the water and opened his eyes. And, for the first time, his eyes filled with light as the bright pool, and bright sky, swirled before him. He let out a whoop of joy, and ran home through the astonished crowds.

"Isn't that the blind beggar, dancing in the streets?" his neighbours asked. "No, it can't be!" They shook their heads in disbelief.

"It's me, all right!" laughed the man born blind.

"How did you get your sight?" they demanded.

"The man called Jesus!"

But his neighbours were troubled, and took him to the Pharisees. They questioned him harshly in the synagogue about what had happened. Some said, "We know this Jesus is not from God, for he breaks the sabbath laws!"

But others said, "If he were bad, how could he do such good things?" And they argued.

Finally, they turned to the man born blind. "Well, they were your eyes he opened – what do you think?"

"He's a prophet, one who speaks and acts for God!" he answered simply.

But still they argued. They even called the man's parents and questioned them.

As these religious leaders argued, the man born blind listened in astonishment. Surely they could see what a great thing had happened to him! He said, "Look, this man opened my eyes. I was blind and now I see. We all know God answers the prayers of those who love and follow him – how could Jesus do such a wonderful thing if he were not from God?"

"How dare you lecture us about God's ways!" cried the Pharisees. "Out! Get out!"

The man born blind sat down outside the place of worship, stunned. Then, someone came up to him.

"Do you believe in the Son of Man – the one sent by God?"

That voice! The man born blind broke into a smile. He knew that voice. It was Jesus.

"I'll believe if you tell me who he is!" he answered.

"You're looking at him right now!"

"I believe!" answered the man.

Jesus noticed the Pharisees listening.

"There's more than one sort of blindness!" Jesus said to them.

"Are you saying we're blind too?" they asked. Jesus studied their faces. These leaders should have been like shepherds to the people, caring for them and feeding them. That is not how they treated the man born blind! So he began talking to them – telling them a parable that was so different from their own knotty arguments.

"When the shepherd comes to the sheepfold, and calls out to his sheep, they'll follow him because they know his voice. They won't follow a stranger. The shepherd will keep them safe from the wolves that howl at night because he loves his sheep. The shepherd leads them to green pasture, and will never abandon them when danger comes – unlike someone hired, who is working for money. The shepherd will lay down his life for his flock.

"I am the good shepherd. I know my sheep, and my sheep know me. They recognize my voice and follow me. And I will lay down my life for them. Some of my sheep are far away – I'll call them, too, and they'll come. They will be one big flock, with one good shepherd."

Yet still the religious leaders argued over who Jesus was. "The man's mad!" said some, while others were less sure. "How can a madman open the eyes of the blind?"

## The found coin and the running father

The Pharisees and the teachers of the Law were not the only ones to be listening to Jesus. He smiled when he saw groups of tax collectors, and others who were considered bad, coming forward.

The Pharisees drew their prayer shawls closer around them. "You see how he welcomes these people – he even eats with them!" They shuddered in disgust. So Jesus wove stories for them, stories that would fill their minds and hearts.

"Suppose a woman has ten silver coins, then loses one. What will she do? She'll light a lamp and sweep the house, turning everything upside down until she finds it. Then she'll call out to her friends, 'I've found it – come and celebrate with me!' That's how it is with God. Every time someone turns away from wrong, and comes to God, the angels celebrate!"

"A man had two sons. One day, the younger one went up to his father and said, 'Father, give me my share of your wealth now!' The father sadly turned over the son's portion of land and money to him. The son's eyes glinted at the sight of all that gold, and soon he was on his way, leaving his family's land without a backward glance.

"He travelled far with his gold, and spent it without a second thought. But when the gold was gone, the wild living and the wine stopped. His new friends sighed when they saw how thin his money bag was, and they slipped away. And just as he was down to his last few coins, the harvest failed. There was nothing to eat. He waited for work with the other landless people in the market, and was hired out by a pig farmer. His hollow stomach ached at the sight of the bean pods in the swill. He began to pick them greedily out of the pigs' trough, but then stopped, straightening himself up.

" 'My father always treats his workers well – they're never hungry. And here I am eating with the pigs!' he said to himself. Then and there he decided to go back home. 'I'll own up to how bad I've been – wronging my father and my God – and ask my father to take me on as a servant. I can't ask to come back as his son.' So he walked away from the pigs and began the long, penniless trudge home. The nearer he got, the more anxious he became. Would his father even want to see him?

"He did not know that every day his father had been watching the road home, waiting, hoping, longing for his return. When the father saw the thin, ragged figure of his son in the distance, he came running, opening his arms wide. The son began his prepared speech: 'Father, I have sinned against God and against you. I'm not worthy to be your son...'

"But the father was laughing, tears rolling down his cheeks. He called over his shoulder to the servants scurrying to keep up. 'Go back, bring him the best clothes, get him some good sandals, and prepare a feast. It's my son! I thought he was dead, but he's alive. He was lost, but now he's found!'

"Now, the older son heard the music and laugher as he made his way home from the fields. 'Your brother's back!' the servants smiled, but the older brother's hands tightened into fists. He would not go in. His father came out to see him.

" 'I've slaved for you for years, and you never threw me a party,' the elder brother growled. 'Now this good-for-nothing son of yours is back, and look – you've roasted him the prize calf!'

" 'Son, everything I have is yours, has always been yours. But we have to celebrate. This brother of yours was dead, and now he's alive; he was lost and now he's found.' "

## The rich man's barns

One day, when Jesus was speaking to the crowds, someone stood up and said, "Teacher, tell my brother to share our inheritance – to divide up the family land fairly!"

Jesus said, "Who gave me the right to divide your property?" Then he said to the crowd, "Watch out for greed – it can sneak up on you. Your life is about much more than what you own.

"Once there was a rich man, whose fields were full of ripe, golden grain, ready to harvest. When it was gathered in, there was so much grain that his barns were creaking and straining with the weight of it. He couldn't store any more. This troubled the farmer – for he wanted to keep it all. 'I know!' he said to himself with a smile. 'I'll tear down these barns and build big new ones, then I'll live the high life! I'll fill my belly and drink my wine and have a good time!'

"But God didn't see it like that. 'You fool! You are going to die tonight – then what will happen to all your fine things? They won't be any use to you then!' "

Jesus looked at the people gathered around him. "That's how it is for anyone who stores up things for themselves, leaving no room for God!"

# Who is my neighbour?

The teacher of the Law stood up, narrowing his eyes in the bright sun. He had heard people talk about Jesus, and now he wanted to test him out.

He pitched his opening question: "Teacher, what must I do to inherit eternal life?"

But Jesus offered the question back to him, giving him the chance to show his knowledge. "What is written in the Law? How do you interpret it?"

The teacher's answer was to quote the scriptures word-for-word: " 'Love the Lord your God with all your soul, strength and mind' and 'Love your neighbour as you love yourself'."

Jesus smiled. "It's a good answer. If you do all that, then you'll have eternal life!"

"But…" the teacher of the Law added in a loud voice, "but who is my neighbour?"

Jesus answered him with a story.

"Once, a man was travelling from Jerusalem to Jericho." The crowd could imagine this journey – the road's steep rocky sides, its twists and turns, its dust and heat. "As he made his way along, a band of robbers crashed down the rocky slope onto the road – they had him surrounded. The man gasped, horrified, but there was nowhere for him to run. They stripped off his clothes and beat him to the ground. They left him lying in the dust, half-dead, while they went to gloat over their takings.

"So there he was, lying helpless in the heat of the sun, when a priest came by. The priest did not stop; he gave the man a wide berth, crossing quickly to the other side. A priest cannot touch blood, or a body – that would make him 'unclean' by Law, unable to work in the Temple, wouldn't it?" Jesus nodded toward the teacher of the Law, then carried on.

"Next came another religious man: a Levite. He, too, saw the man lying bleeding and still. He, too, walked by on the other side, lifting his robes a little to avoid touching the blood on the road, and peering anxiously into the rocky shadows.

"Then, in the distance, came the steady clop of a donkey's hooves. The donkey carried a third man, but this time, he had nothing to do with the Temple. He was a Samaritan." Again he turned to the teacher, who was looking smug now. Samaritans didn't keep to the Law – so he wouldn't know the right thing to do. "The Samaritan saw the broken figure lying bleeding on the road, and his heart was filled with pity. He leaped down, cleaned and soothed his wounds with wine and oil, and tore strips of cloth to make bandages. He slipped his arms under the man and heaved him onto his donkey, leading him gently to an inn. He sat with him all night, giving him sips of water and wine.

"The next day, he spoke to the innkeeper. 'Here are some silver coins. Look after him, and if you spend more, I'll pay you on my return.'"

For a third time Jesus looked at the teacher of the Law, and he asked him, "Now, you answer my question. Which one was a neighbour to the injured man?"

The teacher of the Law shifted uncomfortably. "The one who was kind to him," he answered quietly. Jesus replied, "So go, and do the same!"

## The two sisters

Jesus and his disciples went on their way, and came to the home of Martha and Mary, who were sisters. Martha opened up her home to Jesus, inviting him and his disciples to stay. While she was busy cooking for her guests, Mary went and sat down with the other disciples at Jesus' feet, lost in his words. Meanwhile, Martha was becoming annoyed – getting as hot as her cooking pots. Then, she boiled right over and interrupted Jesus.

"Lord, don't you care that Mary's leaving the work to me? Tell her to come back here and help!"

Jesus spoke gently. "Martha, Martha, you're full of worries – getting so anxious about so many things. But there's only one thing that really matters. And Mary is doing it."

## Stories of the kingdom

Jesus told the people many parables. These stories were full of wisdom about the ways of God – and full, too, of the life people knew.

"The kingdom of heaven is like a farmer who sowed good seed in his field. But one dark night, when all were asleep, an enemy came and sprinkled weed-seeds among the fresh green wheat. When the farmer's servants saw all those weeds coming up in the field, they ran to their master.

" 'Sir! Didn't you sow good seed in your field? How did the weeds get there?'

" 'An enemy did this!' the farmer replied.

" 'Shall we go and pull them up?' the servants asked.

" 'No! If you did that, you'd uproot the wheat shoots, too. Let them grow together until the harvest. Then, bundle up the weeds first and burn them, and bring the wheat into my barns.'

"God's kingdom is like the yeast used in baking. A woman takes a little pinch, and mixes it into a great mound of flour. And the yeast works its way right through the flour, so the dough rises well, making all the bread good." The crowds smiled at the thought of the warm smell of baking.

"Imagine buried treasure. That's what the kingdom of heaven is like. One day, someone was working in a field when they saw something shining. They dug away until they uncovered it all – gold, silver, precious stones. Then they sat back on their heels and laughed with joy. It was a fortune! Quickly, they buried it again and went away. They sold everything they had and bought that one field.

"Or think of a trader looking for fine pearls. At last, he found one that was flawless. It was large, and smooth, and glowed with all the colours of the rainbow. It was the best pearl he had ever seen. He went and sold everything he had, and came back with a heavy purse of gold to buy it."

## The deaf hear and the blind see

And still Jesus travelled from place to place with the good news of God's kingdom, healing the sick. One day, some people brought a man to him – he could hear nothing, and could hardly speak. "Please, Teacher, place your hands on him and heal him!" they said, kneeling at Jesus' feet.

Jesus led him away from the crowds, and then put his fingers in the man's ears. Then he spat and touched the man's tongue. He looked up, and sighed deeply as he said, "Ephphatha!" – which means, "Be opened!"

And the man's ears were opened, and his tongue set free. "Tell no one!" Jesus warned the people, but the man who had been healed could not keep quiet.

Soon, everyone knew. "Everything Jesus does is good!" they said. "He even makes the deaf hear and the mute speak!"

At Bethsaida, people brought a blind man to him. Once again, he led the man away from the crowds. He spat on the man's eyes and put his hands on him. He asked, "Do you see anything?"

The man replied, "I see people, but they look like walking trees!" Once more, Jesus put his hands on the man, and his eyes opened wide, letting in the light. He could now see everything clearly.

# WHO IS JESUS?

## *What do you think?*

The disciples whispered uneasily as they followed Jesus north, away from Galilee. They reached a green, wooded place, under the shadow of the great rock where the city of Caesarea Philippi had been built to honour the great Roman emperor, Caesar Augustus. The city was so different from home. Here, the crowds did not follow them. Why had Jesus come to such a place?

They sat down in the deep shade of the silver-leaved olive trees, and rested. Jesus asked a question: "Who do people say I am?"

They answered, "Some say you are John the Baptist back from the dead. Others, that you are Elijah, or Jeremiah, or another great prophet from long ago." The disciples lowered their heads, remembering how John had been beheaded on the orders of the king.

"But what do you think? Who do you say I am?" For a moment their silence continued, and nothing could be heard but the gentle sound of crickets in the warm air. Then Simon spoke.

"You are the Christ, the Messiah, Son of the living God!"

Jesus smiled. "You are blessed by God, Simon! You didn't learn this answer from anyone else; the truth was revealed to you by God himself. From now on I'll call you Peter, the Rock, and on this good, solid rock I'll build my church. Not even death will be able to overcome my church. And I give you the keys of the kingdom of heaven, too."

Then, Jesus looked down the valley at the little stream that would grow into the Jordan and flow south through the land. He spoke gently, telling them that he, too, must go south, following the long road to Jerusalem. The disciples gasped, dismayed, as he told them that he would be handed over to the chief priests and killed. They shook their heads, not understanding, when he spoke of being raised to life on the third day. And what did Jesus mean when he spoke of taking up a cross, and of his glory?

## Changed before their eyes

Jesus led his disciples on from Caesarea Philippi toward higher ground. Jesus took Simon Peter, James, and John, and began to climb the steep slopes of a mountain that rose above the landscape. Rocks slid under their feet as they walked under the bright, burning sun. At last they reached the top, and looked down on the outstretched wings of eagles rising through the hot, shimmering air.

And there, under the wide, open sky, Jesus was transformed before their eyes. He was shining, changed, his clothes dazzling white – brighter than pure, untrodden mountain snow. Then, the disciples saw two figures join Jesus – Moses, the Law-giver, and Elijah, the prophet. And there, on that high mountain, they talked together.

Simon Peter, James, and John watched wide-eyed until Simon Peter said, "Rabbi, Teacher, it's so good for us to be here. Let us build shelters for you, and Moses, and Elijah."

Then cloud swirled around them, and a voice came from the cloud. "This is my Son, the one I love. Listen to him!" Then there was silence, and they were alone with Jesus.

On the steep path back down, Jesus turned to them and said, "Don't tell anyone what you have seen until I have risen from the dead!" And the three whispered together, wondering what rising from the dead might mean.

## Zacchaeus

Jesus made his way steadily toward Jerusalem. On his way he passed through Jericho, with its date palms and fragrant balsam trees. Crowds poured out to see him, and to see a blind beggar Jesus had just healed by the roadside.

"What's all the commotion? Come away from there and get on with your work!" Zacchaeus, the chief tax collector of the region, called out to his assistants. They scurried back to their work, and the quiet clink of gold coins. But Zacchaeus could not concentrate – the joy of the crowd had unsettled him. He swept neat heaps of gold into his purse and went out.

The sounds got louder and louder. The crowds were calling out for Jesus. Zacchaeus tried to catch a glimpse of the Teacher, but he could not, for he was a short man, and the people would not let him through. He ran on ahead and shinned up the stout trunk of a sycamore fig tree, sliding out along one of the branches that shaded the road. Then he waited, watching Jesus getting closer, as he talked and laughed with the people. Suddenly, quite close to the tree, Jesus stopped, and looked up. Zacchaeus gasped, and tried to hide among the leaves. Everyone was looking now.

"Zacchaeus, isn't it?" Jesus said. "You'd better hurry down from there. I'd like to stay at your house today!" So the chief tax collector swung down, rubbing green smears from his fine robes. They set off together, and Zacchaeus threw open his doors to Jesus and his friends, beaming with joy.

But the crowds were spitting with anger. "Did you see that? He's gone to be a guest of that thief, that collaborator with the Romans!"

Zacchaeus stood up before them all, and spoke to Jesus. "Look, Lord, I'll give half of everything I have to the poor right now! And if I've cheated anyone, I'll pay them back four times over!"

Jesus answered, "God's power is at work in this house today – the power to rescue and to change. This man, too, is one of God's children. For the Son of Man came to seek, and to save, those who have lost the way to God!"

## Jesus and Lazarus

Jesus followed the road on toward Jerusalem, stopping at the desert place by the Jordan where John had baptized him: where the sky had opened and the Spirit had come down like a dove. Many people came to him there, and many believed. While he was by the Jordan, a messenger arrived.

"Teacher, I bring word from Martha and Mary of Bethany. Your dear friend, their brother Lazarus, is very ill."

"This sickness will not end in death, but in God's glory!" Jesus replied. But he did not follow the messenger back. Two days later, he stood up and turned to his disciples.

"Come on, let's go!" he said. But they were afraid to go so close to Jerusalem, remembering how Jesus' life was in danger there.

He stepped forward onto the sun-baked road. "Now it's daylight. Lazarus is asleep, and I'm going to wake him up!" And the disciples followed Jesus, despite their fears.

As they came close to Bethany, they saw Martha running toward them. "Lord," she called out, "if you had been here, my brother would not have died." Sobbing shook her as Jesus stepped toward her, steadying her. "But I know," she carried on, quietly, "even now, God would do anything you asked."

"Your brother will rise again," Jesus said.

"Yes, I know, on the Last Day – the day of resurrection, of new life."

"I am the resurrection, I am the life. Whoever believes in me will live, and will never be swallowed up by the dark emptiness of death. Do you believe this?"

"Yes, Lord, I believe you are the Christ, the Son of God, who was promised from long ago!" Then she went back to find Mary.

"Sister, the Teacher is here!" Straight away Mary got up and went out, followed by those who had come to mourn with her. She went up to Jesus and fell weeping at his feet.

"Lord!" she said. "If you had been here, my brother would not have died!" Jesus saw her sorrow, and looked at those around, draped in black and weeping. And he, too, shuddered under the heavy weight of grief.

"Where is he?" Jesus asked.

"Come and see, Lord," they answered.

And Jesus wept. "See how much he loved him!" said some.

"Could he not then have saved him?" questioned others.

They came before the tomb – a cave with a stone rolled across the entrance.

"Take away the stone!" Jesus said, but Martha hesitated.

"Lord, he has been dead four days. The body will smell," she said.

"If you believe, you will see God's glory!" Jesus answered, and they rolled the stone away. He prayed in a loud voice, and then he looked into the deep darkness of the tomb. "Lazarus, come out!" he called. And Lazarus came out, wrapped in linen grave clothes, with a cloth around his face. "Set him free from his grave clothes!" Jesus said to those around him, who stared in astonishment as the man they had been mourning stood before them, alive again.

## The plot against Jesus

Many had come from Jerusalem to comfort Martha and Mary in their grief – and these people saw what had taken place at the tomb. Many put their faith in Jesus, but some went back to the city and told the Pharisees, the religious leaders, what had happened. A meeting of the Sanhedrin, the ruling council, was called.

"Something must be done. If the people stop listening to us and listen to Jesus instead, we'll lose everything! The Romans will take away our power, our rights in the Temple. The whole Jewish nation could be finished!"

Then Caiaphas, the high priest, spoke. "It would be better if one man died for the sake of the people, rather than risk losing the whole nation."

And from then on, the religious leaders plotted to take Jesus' life. But still, as the crowds began to arrive in Jerusalem for the Passover, they asked, "Where is Jesus? Isn't he coming for the feast?"

# Poured out

At Bethany, Martha gave a dinner in honour of Jesus, with Lazarus by his side. "How can we thank you? Our brother is restored to us!" Martha said, her eyes shining bright in the lamplight. For in that house, there were no more tears.

Then Mary came in carrying a jar of pure nard, the rich smell of the precious perfume swirling around her. She knelt down at Jesus' feet and poured the nard over them, wiping them with her hair. The heady scent spread and filled the whole house.

But Judas Iscariot, one of the Twelve, who looked after the money, was angry. "We could have sold that perfume and given the money to the poor – it was worth a year's wages!"

Jesus silenced him. "Leave her alone. The perfume is for my burial. There will always be poor people – but you will not always have me."

Outside the house, a crowd had gathered from Jerusalem to see Jesus and also to see Lazarus, who had been raised from the dead. Many people were following Jesus because of what he had done for Lazarus, and the chief priests were angrier than ever.

# Into Jerusalem

The next day, word spread that Jesus was going to enter Jerusalem. People poured out of the gates, and those who were with him gathered, waiting to see what would happen. Jesus sat on a young donkey, and began the ride toward the city as people cut palm branches from the trees and went out to meet him on the road. The crowds were bursting with joy – shouting and cheering to see Jesus, at last, coming into Jerusalem. They remembered God's promises from long ago, and they believed their eyes would see them fulfilled.

"Hosanna – God saves!" they cried. "Blessed is the one who comes in the name of the Lord!" "Blessed is the king of Israel!"

The disciples followed, astonished, and laughing with joy. At last, the kingdom was coming.

But there were those in the city who looked down from shadowy windows, and would not listen to the words of those who had seen Jesus raise Lazarus from the dead. They drew back from the laughing, shining crowds that poured through the open gates in dazzling sunshine. The Pharisees were afraid. They said, "Look, the whole world is following him now!"

Jesus tried to explain that his kingdom was not as his followers expected, and tried to warn them of his death. "You are going to have the light with you for only a little while longer. Walk while you have the light, before the darkness overwhelms you. Put your trust in the light."

## Jesus at the Temple

Jesus went into the Temple courts, and found them choked up with stalls and salesmen, ringing with the shouts of hawkers and hagglers. People were not gathering for worship: they were changing their money into special Temple coins, and buying birds for Temple offerings. Jesus grabbed the traders' tables, and threw them over. The money changers and the dove sellers shouted angrily while the coins clattered and rolled across the stone floor. "You've taken 'the house of prayer' and turned it into a 'den of thieves'!" Jesus said, and all fell silent at his words.

Then, the blind and the lame came to him and were healed.

And children came, too, running and shouting, "Hosanna to the Son of David!" The Temple was filled with joy, and the priests and teachers of the Law drew back, muttering angrily.

## Teaching in the Temple

The teachers of the Law challenged Jesus, and tried to catch him out with their arguments. Once again, he replied to their arguments in parables.

"A man planted a fine vineyard, with a wine press and a watchtower, but he had to go away before the first grapes were ripe. So he left his vineyard in the care of tenants. When it was harvest time, he sent a servant back to collect a share of the grapes, but the tenants beat him and threw him out with nothing. So the landowner sent another servant, but the tenants struck him over the head and sent him away empty-handed. Again and again this happened, and each time the tenants killed or beat the landlord's servant.

"Then, in the end, the landlord sent his son, whom he loved. 'They'll respect him, surely!' the landlord thought. But they did not. They killed him and threw him out, hoping greedily for his inheritance.

"Do you think they got it? No, of course not! The owner came back, killed the tenants, and handed the vineyard over to others."

The teachers of the Law knew Jesus had cast them as the tenants in this parable. How they seethed, longing to arrest him. But they were afraid. So they tried to think of other ways to trip him up in front of everyone in the Temple courts.

"Teacher," one of them began. "We know you follow the ways of God, that you speak the truth. So, should we pay taxes to the Roman emperor or not?" Jesus was saddened by the cunning glint in his eyes.

"Have you a coin I could look at?" he said, patting his empty money bag. The man held one out.

"Whose portrait is this, and the writing – who is it about?" Jesus asked.

"The emperor!" replied the man. Now, the Jews were allowed special coins, which bore no image of the emperor, for use in the Temple. This coin was a standard Roman one.

"Well then, give to the emperor what is the emperor's, and give to God what is God's!"

People were astonished at his answers.

"Which of the many commands is the most important?" asked one of the teachers.

"This is the most important," said Jesus. " 'Love the Lord your God with all your heart and soul and might.' The second is, 'Love your neighbour as you love yourself.' That's it. Nothing else comes close!" The teacher smiled.

"Yes, of course. To love God like that, and to love your neighbour like that, matters more than all the burned offerings and sacrifices of this Temple!"

"You are not far from the kingdom of God!" smiled Jesus. And from then on, the trap setters were quiet.

Jesus sat and watched the crowds putting money in the Temple treasury. Many rich people came, and threw in handfuls of silver and gold that glinted in the sunlight. Then came a poor widow, who slipped in two small, dull copper coins.

"Did you see that?" Jesus asked the disciples. "She put in more than all the others!" The disciples raised their eyebrows. Jesus continued, "The others gave part of their great wealth – she gave all she had to live on. She gave everything!"

# The last meal

"Master, where shall we go to prepare for the Passover?" the disciples asked. For Jerusalem was bustling with people getting ready for the Passover feast, when the Jewish people remembered how they were brought out of slavery in Egypt, and into freedom.

"Go – you will meet someone who will give you a room." And they did. It was just as Jesus said.

# The servant king

Evening came, and Jesus and his disciples were together in the upper room they had been given. Jesus knew the time had come for him to leave the world – and those he loved, and would love to the end. Jesus knew that God had given him power over all things, and so he took a towel, and tied it around his waist. He knelt down before his followers, and began washing their feet.

"No, Lord!" burst out Simon Peter when Jesus came to him. "I can't let you do that!"

"You don't understand yet – to be part of me, you must let me serve you."

"Then wash my hands and my head, too," Simon Peter replied.

Jesus came to Judas. He knew that Judas had already agreed to betray him to the high priests and the Temple guard, but still, he carried on washing his feet.

"Do you understand?" Jesus said when he had finished. "I'm your Teacher, your Lord, and yet I take the place of the humblest slave. So you also must serve each other, and you will be blessed in doing so."

# Bread and wine

Then they began the Passover meal. They ate flat bread with bitter leaves, and dipped greens in salt water, to remember the bitterness and the tears of slavery in Egypt. Once more, they told each other the story of how God saved the people of Israel. But then, Jesus' face clouded with sadness.

"One of you is going to betray me!" he said.

"No!" they all answered, pale with shock.

"One who shares my bread," Jesus said, giving a piece to Judas.

While they were eating, Jesus took the bread, gave thanks, and broke it, giving it to all of them saying, "Take and eat, for it is my body." Then, after supper, he raised the cup, and gave thanks. "Drink, all of you. For this is my blood, poured out for forgiveness. It is the blood of the new covenant – the binding promise of God."

During the meal, Judas slipped out unnoticed into the dark, dark night.

"Now the glory begins, and I give you a new command. You must love one another. Your lives will be marked by love, and all will know you are mine because of it. For I will leave you, and you cannot follow yet," Jesus said.

"I'll follow you anywhere!" said Simon Peter.

"Will you? Before the cock crows, you will deny three times you even knew me."

They were all silent, stricken with sadness.

"You are troubled – don't be. Think of it like this. I'm going ahead to my Father's house, to get rooms ready for you. Then I'll come back for you. You know the way!"

Thomas said, "We don't know where you're going, and we don't know the way!"

"I am the way," said Jesus. And his disciples remembered the many long, dusty roads they had followed him along. Now, where would they go, what would they do? He saw their sadness, and spoke gently to them for a long time, giving them hope.

"I am a vine, and from me grow branches – you. The vine gives the branches life, and they bud and blossom and fruit. So draw your life from me, and you will bud and blossom and fruit too.

"When I go, the Spirit will come, to guide you into all truth. In this world, you will face trouble. But take courage: I have overcome the world!"

## Gethsemane

They went out from Jerusalem to the Mount of Olives and, in the darkness, came to Gethsemane, the olive grove. "Wait here while I pray!" Jesus said – but he took Simon Peter, James, and John with him, further among the trees. There, deep in the cold night shadows, Jesus shuddered.

"This sorrow – it's flooding me, drowning me. Keep watch with me." And he went on a few more steps, then fell to the ground. "Abba, my Father, take this bitter cup from me… but please, what happens must be what you want, and not what I want." He drew himself up, and went back to the disciples, but they had fallen asleep. Again he prayed, and again; and each time the disciples were overcome with deep sleep. They could not stay awake with him.

"Still sleeping? Get up! My betrayer is here!"

For now Judas was coming, with a crowd bearing swords and clubs. Orange torchlight flickered on the silver leaves, making twisted, jumping shadows. Judas stepped forward. "Rabbi!" he said, and he kissed the one he called Teacher. As Jesus was seized by the armed men, his disciples finally roused themselves, drawing swords and shouting.

But Jesus said, "Do you think I am leading a rebellion? Is that why you have come for me like this – at night, with your swords drawn? I was with you every day in the Temple. You heard me teaching, and did nothing. But it must be so. The prophecies must be fulfilled."

Then his followers drew back between the trees, and fled into the darkness.

## Accused

Simon Peter followed, watching, as Jesus walked steadily between the angry armed men who led him to the high priest's house. Jesus was taken inside, leaving Simon Peter in the courtyard, where a bright fire was kindled against the cold. Simon Peter sat down with the guards, stretching out his numb hands toward the orange light.

He shifted uncomfortably as he felt the gaze of a servant girl fall on him. "This man was with him!" she said, for they had been talking of Jesus.

"I don't know him!" Simon Peter replied, shrinking back.

Then a man spoke out from the shadows, "You are one of his followers."

"I am not!" Simon Peter snapped.

Later, another said, "You must have been with him – you're from Galilee, aren't you?"

"I don't know what you are talking about!" Simon Peter blustered, as the cock crowed in the thin light before dawn. Then he remembered what Jesus had said, and went outside, and wept bitterly.

At the same time, as dawn was breaking, the council gathered – elders, chief priests, teachers of the Law – and faced Jesus.

"If you are the Christ, the Promised One, then tell us!" one said, rolling the words around his mouth as if they were bitter to his taste.

"If I told you, you would not believe me," Jesus replied, holding him in his steady gaze.

"Are you the Son of God?" they asked.

"You are right to say so."

At this they rose to their feet with an angry roar, and carried Jesus off to the palace of Pilate, the Roman governor, who had power to sentence people to death.

"This man is a threat to the peace – he claims to be Christ, a king, and opposes Roman taxes," the accusers called out as Pilate circled around Jesus.

"Are you the King of the Jews?" he asked. Jesus felt the cold edges of the mosaic under his bare feet.

"Yes," he replied. "But my kingdom is not like the kingdoms of this world."

"So, you are a king!" Pilate responded.

"Yes! That is why I came, to speak the truth. Everyone who is on the side of truth will listen to me."

"But what is truth?" Pilate asked. Then he went out to see the leaders and the people together. "I see no reason to charge him," Pilate said. "This man has done nothing to deserve death. I will set him free."

"No, set Barabbas free instead!" they cried. Now, Barabbas was a rebel against the Romans who had killed a man.

They shouted louder, drowning out Pilate's words: "He's done nothing wrong! I will release him!"

But, with rising rage, the mob shouted, "Crucify, crucify!" In the end, Pilate gave in: he set Barabbas free and handed Jesus over to the guards.

The guards tormented Jesus, the one called king. They draped a fine, purple robe around him, and twisted him a crown of sharp thorns to wear. They called out, "Hail, King of the Jews!" and fell on their knees before him, laughing. They spat on him, and struck his head with a staff. Then, they took back the robe, and led him out to be crucified in his own simple clothes.

## The road of tears and the place of the skull

Jesus stumbled under the heavy wooden cross, weak from his beating. The soldiers looked up at the crowds and saw a strong man making his way into the city from the country. It was Simon, a visitor from Cyrene in North Africa. They ordered Simon to pick up the cross and carry it behind Jesus as he walked slowly over the rough, hard road.

A large crowd followed behind Jesus and Simon, and among them were many women, sobbing. Jesus turned to them and said, "Daughters of Jerusalem, do not weep for me. You and your children will know enough pain."

Two other men were led out to be crucified with Jesus at Golgotha, the Place of the Skull: one on his left, and one on his right. So Jesus was nailed to the cross, and a sign was hung above him, saying: "This is the King of the Jews."

From the cross, Jesus spoke slowly, painfully. "Father, forgive them, for they do not know what they are doing."

But some among the crowd sneered, "Save yourself if you really are chosen by God. You saved others!"

The soldiers joined in, as did one of the men being crucified with Jesus. But the other said, "Don't you fear God, at the hour of your death? We are guilty, but this man has done nothing wrong." He turned his head toward Jesus. "Jesus, remember me when you come into your kingdom!"

And Jesus answered, "Today, you will be with me in paradise."

Then, a deep darkness came over the land, and the shadows spread and joined together. In the Temple, the curtain that hid the holiest place – the Holy of Holies – was torn in two. "Father, take my spirit!" Jesus called in a loud voice, and then his head fell forward, and his breath stopped.

The Roman centurion at the foot of the cross said, "Surely this was a good man." And many of the crowd were overcome by sadness, and turned away. But those who knew him, men and women, stayed, and kept watch.

## The tomb

Joseph of Arimathea, a secret follower of Jesus, went to see Pilate. "I request permission to bury Jesus," he said, and Pilate gave him the body. So Joseph and Nicodemus, the man who had visited Jesus at night, took Jesus away. Nicodemus had brought a great weight of spices – myrrh and aloes – and together the two men prepared Jesus' body with the spices and wrapped it in linen. Then they carried him to Joseph's garden tomb, cut into the rock, and there they laid him. They rolled the stone over the entrance, shutting out the last red rays of light. Then they turned, and walked away. But Mary Magdalene, who had been healed by Jesus, and the other Mary stayed and kept watch in the chill of the deepening shadows.

# NEW LIFE

## Where is he?

The door was locked, the shutters were closed over the windows, and a faint lamp smoked fitfully in the corner. Jesus' followers hardly dared speak: they hardly dared breathe. As they sat in the small room where they had all gathered after the night of the crucifixion, they hung their heads. The shock of Jesus' death had stunned them, and fear for their own lives kept them shut away behind locked doors.

But now, it was near morning on the third day after Jesus had died, and Mary Magdalene began to watch the crack in the shutters for the faintest glimpse of new light. When she could wait no longer she slipped out of the house, keeping to the deepest shadows, and ran to the place where she had kept watch – the place where Jesus was buried.

Then, she stopped. The stone covering the entrance of the cave-tomb had been rolled away – who could have done it? She ran back to the others. "He's gone – they've taken him!" she gasped. Simon Peter and John raced to the tomb ahead of her. They saw the strips of linen, and the burial cloth, but there was no body. The men ran back to Jerusalem, but Mary stayed, weeping, exhausted, and bent low.

Then she looked into the tomb. She saw two angels in white,

seated where the body had been. Their voices were strong, yet gentle. "Woman, why do you cry?"

"They've taken my Lord away, and I don't know where he is!" she answered. Then she straightened, and turned, seeing a man through her tears.

"Woman, why are you crying? Who are you looking for?"

Mary thought he must be the gardener, beginning his work in the cool dawn. "Have you taken him, sir? Tell me where he is, and I'll go and get him."

"Mary!" said the man. And Mary knew his voice. It was Jesus, standing there before her. Alive!

"My Teacher!" she called, reaching out.

"Don't hold onto me – go back and tell my brothers, my disciples, that I am returning to my Father and their Father, my God and their God."

She stepped backwards and then ran, as dawn began to colour the sky. She threw open the door to the room where the disciples were hidden, and pale, golden light washed over their faces. She called out, "I have seen the Lord!" Her voice rang loud in the still room and her eyes were wide with wonder, but they did not know how to answer her.

## On the road

Two of Jesus' followers left Jerusalem that day, walking to the village of Emmaus. While they walked, they began to talk about all that had happened. And as they shared their grief and bewilderment, Jesus joined them and walked with them. But they did not know who he was.

"What are you talking about?" he asked.

They stopped, and stood still on the white, dusty road. "Are you the only one from Jerusalem who doesn't know what's been going on?" said Cleopas.

"Tell me!" said Jesus.

"There was a prophet called Jesus of Nazareth, a true man of God. But the chief priests handed him over to be killed, and he was crucified." Cleopas paused. "We had hoped he was the one God had promised from long ago. But then... today, some of the women went to the tomb and came back saying it was empty, and that Jesus was alive!" For a moment, hope glimmered in Cleopas's eyes, and then he shook his head.

"But don't you see?" Jesus said. "Haven't you read the teachings of the prophets? Don't you know that these things had to happen?" And so he began to explain. It was as if he were unrolling scroll after scroll along the road before them – all the Law, and all the teachings of the prophets – letting them see that the Messiah had to suffer and die and rise again.

"Stay with us, it's getting dark!" the pair said as they came to Emmaus. So Jesus stayed at their home. Then, at the table, he took bread, and blessed it, and broke it to share with them. In that breaking and sharing of bread, their eyes were suddenly opened and, with a gasp, they recognized it was Jesus who sat before them. But then he slipped from their sight.

"Did you feel it too, as we walked along? That burning – that deep, rising joy – that sudden understanding?" they asked each other as they grabbed their cloaks. And they set off back to their friends in Jerusalem through the thickening darkness, laughing with joy, and leaving their supper on the table.

## Behind locked doors

When evening came on the third day after Jesus died, the disciples
were talking together behind locked doors. Then, suddenly, as they
were still talking, Jesus was there among them. "Peace be with
you!" he said, as he showed them his wounds. Then, they were
all filled with such joy, for they all saw that Jesus really was alive.

All, that is, but Thomas, who was not with them that evening.
"I'll not believe it!" he said when they told him they had seen
Jesus. "No! Not unless I see the nail marks in his hands with my
own eyes, and touch the wound on his side." For Jesus had been
pierced by a Roman spear while he hung on the cross.

For a week Thomas ignored the wild talk of "rising from the
dead". But then he had a chance to see for himself. Once again,
the disciples were together behind locked doors, hiding from the
Temple guard. And Jesus came and stood among them and said,
"Peace be with you!" Then he turned to Thomas, opening his
hands. "Put your finger here in my hands, and here, at my side.
Let go of your doubts and believe!"

And Thomas, believing, replied, "My Lord, and my God!"

## Fishing in Galilee

Jesus' followers remembered he had said that he would go on to
Galilee, and so, when the Passover celebrations were ending, they
slipped out of Jerusalem among the crowds of pilgrims who were
going home. Then, they took the road north, and waited.

They strolled along the shores of Lake Galilee, feeling the
cool, watery breeze, watching the boats bobbing gently. They
remembered the life they had before Jesus called them.

"I'm going fishing!" said Simon Peter.

"We'll come with you!" replied the others. And they pushed the old boat out into the water, and spent the night casting their nets under a bright moon. Each time they pulled the nets up, they were empty. So, when dawn came, their heads hung low.

"Good morning!" called a voice from the shore. "Haven't you caught anything then?"

"No!" came the short reply.

"Throw the net over the right side of the boat. Then you'll find fish!" There was something about that voice… So the disciples went ahead and threw the net over the right side of the boat. Then they grabbed the ropes, and heaved. They braced their backs, and heaved again. They could not lift the net – it was so full of fish!

"It's Jesus," John said in a whisper, and Simon Peter leaped overboard, swimming and splashing to the figure on the shore. The others inched forward in the boat, towing the heavy, writhing net behind them.

As Simon Peter emerged, dripping, from the water, he saw Jesus sitting by a fire, roasting silver fish on the hot stones, and the warm smell of fresh bread filled him with hunger. "Bring me some more fish – ones you have caught!" Jesus asked, so he did.

"Come and have breakfast with me!" Jesus said, so they sat around the fire together, as they had done so many times before. Jesus broke the bread and gave it to them, then he did the same with the fish.

After they had finished eating, Jesus turned to Simon Peter. In the distance a cock crowed, and the fisherman looked down at the ground.

"Simon, do you love me?" Jesus asked.

"Yes, Lord. You know that!" Simon Peter answered.

"Then feed my lambs." And again he asked, "Simon, do you love me?"

"Yes, Lord. You know I love you."

"Take care of my sheep." A third time he asked, "Simon, do you love me?"

"Lord, you know everything! Surely you know how I love you!"

"Feed my sheep!" came Jesus' reply. Then he talked to Simon Peter about the things that would happen to him in years to come, and about the kind of death Simon Peter would die.

Then Jesus said, "Follow me!"

## Taken up

The disciples never knew when Jesus would appear among them – but appear he did, telling them more about the kingdom of God, and kindling hope in their hearts.

"Wait in Jerusalem and you will receive God's gift. You remember how John baptized with water? In a few days, you will be baptized with the Holy Spirit of God."

Another time they asked him, "Lord, will Israel be a great kingdom again now?"

"That's not for you to know. The Holy Spirit will come and fill you with power, and then you will tell everyone what you have seen and heard. Start in Jerusalem, and Judea, but then go out beyond Israel to Samaria, and even further – to the whole earth!"

Then Jesus was lifted up, above and beyond the earth, and a cloud hid him. The disciples stood and stared, craning their necks.

"Men of Galilee, why are you staring up into the sky?" They

turned to see who was speaking. It was two men, dressed in white, who were standing with them. "Jesus has been taken from you to heaven, and one day he will come back!"

So the disciples walked from the Mount of Olives to Jerusalem to wait, as Jesus had said. They chose one of the disciples, Matthias, to join the Twelve. For now, only eleven were left. Judas, the betrayer, overcome with guilt, had ended his own life. Now, at last, they understood that the kingdom had not ended with the death of Jesus, and that the work of spreading the kingdom was becoming theirs.

## The Spirit comes

From the fields it came: the first sheaf of barley cut for that year's harvest. It was carried high through streets crammed with visitors, and on to the Temple. And then the priests offered it to God, giving thanks for the good land, and for the gift of harvest. For that day was the celebration of the first fruits. It was Pentecost.

Meanwhile, the disciples were all together, waiting. Then, suddenly, it began. It started with sound – a sound like the wind – but this was no gentle harvest breeze. This was a shaking and a roaring: a sound of power, whooshing and howling about the house, rattling every door and shutter. The sound seemed to come down from heaven itself, and filled the house as the wind fills sails. Then, the disciples watched wide-eyed as something that looked like fire came down, and tongues of flame peeled off it and rested on each one of them without burning them. All of them were filled, for the Holy Spirit had come. And as it happened, their tongues were loosened, and they began to speak as the Spirit gave them words. These words were not Aramaic, their own language, but in languages that were unknown to them.

A crowd had gathered by the house because of the extraordinary sound, but then they heard the voices. There were pilgrims in Jerusalem from all over the known world, and they recognized the words the disciples were speaking.

"He's talking Egyptian!" said one.

"That one's talking my language," said a visitor from Crete – and the same was true for all. Each person heard God's praises in their own tongue.

"What can it mean?" they asked each other. But others among the crowd joked that the disciples had been drinking.

The Twelve heard what they were saying, so Simon Peter stood up to speak to the crowds.

"Listen, I'll tell you what's happening. We're not drunk! It's too early in the day for that! This is God's promise come true. Don't you remember what one of the prophets wrote long ago?

> " 'I'll pour out my Spirit on everyone –
> young and old. Your sons and daughters will prophesy,
> young men will have visions, and old men dreams.
> All who follow me – men and women – will
> be given my Spirit, and there will be wonders!'

"Listen, I'm going to tell you about Jesus. The one who worked wonders among us; the one you handed over to be killed on a cross. He's alive – he's been raised from the dead. We've seen him!"

A gasp rose up from the crowd at Simon Peter's words, and some began to weep, for now they could see that Jesus was the Promised One.

"What shall we do?" they asked.

"Turn away from wrong. Be baptized. You'll find forgiveness, and you'll receive this great gift – the Holy Spirit. It's a promise for you and your children, and for all those whom God is calling from far away!" And that day, about 3,000 were baptized, and joined Jesus' followers.

It was an extraordinary community. People hung on every word spoken by those who had known Jesus, and they lived closely, like a family. They shared their possessions, and they broke bread together. No one was hungry or poor. They were respected by everyone, and every day people were drawn to them. Every day, they gave thanks to God.

## In the name of Jesus

Jesus' followers went to the Temple to worship every day. Once, Simon Peter and John were making their way to one of the main gates – the Beautiful Gate – when they saw a man being carried to the place where he would sit and beg. The man was lowered down on to the dusty ground, his feet awkward and useless before him. "Look at us!" Simon Peter said. The man gave them all his attention, hoping for money. "I have no silver or gold for you," Simon Peter went on. "But I give what I do have – in the name of Jesus Christ of Nazareth, walk!"

He took the man's hand in his own and helped him up. The beggar felt his ankles and feet growing strong under him. "God is good!" he shouted, and he began to test out his healed feet, walking, leaping, dancing, and praising God through the Temple colonnades.

Everyone came running to see what was happening, wide-eyed with surprise.

"Why does this amaze you?" Simon Peter asked. "Why do you stare as if we did this ourselves? We didn't. This is God's power, working through Jesus, whom you crucified. It's in his name, and by faith in him, that this healing has come!" And Simon Peter persuaded many to join them, talking of how Jesus was raised from the dead.

But the priests, and the Temple guard, and the Sadducees – who did not believe in angels, or eternal life – came up to challenge Simon Peter and John. They put them in jail, and the next day they were questioned.

"Are we on trial for an act of kindness?" Simon Peter asked. "We did this in the name of Jesus Christ, the one you had crucified, but who is alive again!"

The leaders muttered anxiously. They were afraid. "Don't do anything in this name any more – stop talking about that man!" they ordered.

"Should we obey you, or God?" Simon Peter and John answered. They spoke with such power that the leaders were troubled. So they threatened them and sent them away.

When Simon Peter and John told the rest of the believers what had happened, they prayed together: "Great and mighty God, who made all things, give us courage to speak in your name, through Jesus. Heal and save, do wonders!"

And that is what happened. The kingdom grew and spread, and many were brought to the disciples for healing, as they had been brought to Jesus.

# Anger

The leaders of the Jewish people watched with horror as the Temple was filled with the healed, listening to fishermen and tax collectors telling them about God, telling them that Jesus was the Messiah. This man's disciples were everywhere, and people were listening to them. Again, the religious leaders tried to arrest Jesus' disciples, but the disciples spoke with such power that the religious leaders could do nothing against them.

The number of disciples grew and grew, and there were some among them who were poor and hungry. Seven good people were chosen to make sure the food was shared out fairly, and Stephen was one of them. He was a man full of God's Spirit, and many wonders were done through him. The Temple leaders tried to argue with Stephen, but were stunned silent by his wisdom. So they plotted and schemed, and got people to tell lies about him. They brought him to trial, where he spoke with power, explaining how Jesus was the key to God's great plan for the Jewish people, and saying that the religious leaders were guilty of his death.

All their anger, all their jealousy, was then unleashed against Stephen. He stood still, not hearing their bitter words. "Look!" he said. "Heaven's opening up – Jesus is standing at the right hand of God, ready to welcome me!"

They covered their ears and roared, dragging him out of the city. There, they stoned him, and, as the hard rocks struck him again and again, he prayed, "Lord Jesus, take my spirit. Don't hold this sin against them!"

And a man called Saul was there, looking after the cloaks of the stone throwers, approving of Stephen's death.

They did not stop there. Saul went back into the city, going from house to house dragging out men and women who followed Jesus. Many ran, scattering across the land. But wherever they went, they talked of Jesus. Philip, one of the Twelve, ran to Samaria, where he healed the sick, and set people free from evil. Many Samaritans believed when they saw the miracles, and word reached Simon Peter and John. They hurried out from Jerusalem, their minds full of the words Jesus spoke before he was taken up to heaven – that God's kingdom must spread out beyond Judea. So they prayed that the Samaritans would receive the Holy Spirit, too, and receive it they did.

Then, Philip moved on again. He went south, on the desert road to Gaza. A fine chariot was travelling along, and Philip was drawn to it and ran alongside. He could hardly believe what he heard: someone was reading out loud from the book of the prophet Isaiah. It was the very passage where Isaiah talks of the Promised One: "He was led like a sheep to the slaughter…" Philip looked at the man reading, scroll unfurling across his lap. He was an official of the queen of Ethiopia, returning to Africa.

"Do you understand what you're reading?" Philip asked, panting.

"How can I, unless someone explains it?" the Ethiopian answered, stopping the chariot. So Philip climbed in, and explained how Jesus died, and rose again, and then the man believed that Jesus was the one Isaiah had spoken of.

"Look, here is water!" the Ethiopian said. "Could I be baptized?" And Philip baptized him. Already, the good news was spilling out of Jerusalem like wine from a split wineskin.

# Saul is changed

"I must go to Damascus. I must root out followers of that man Jesus there, too!" Saul spat the words out angrily as he paced the floor in front of the high priest, anxious to travel north after the new, fast-spreading faith. The high priest gave him letters of authority to seize and imprison any of Jesus' followers found in Damascus, and Saul set off with them strapped tightly in his saddle bag.

It was a long road. But before they reached the city, Saul was stopped in his tracks.

It was a bolt from the blue, a dazzling white light that flashed around him. He fell to the ground as a voice called out, "Saul, Saul, why are you persecuting me?"

"Who are you, Lord?"

"I am Jesus, the one you are hurting," the voice said. "Now get up and go into the city. You will be told what to do."

The men travelling with Saul had stood back, bewildered. They had heard a sound, but what could it mean? And then, when Saul stood up and tried to open his eyes, he could see nothing. So they led him slowly through the city gates, and he spent three days in darkness, not eating, and not drinking. He had been so sure that he was doing the right thing. But now, alone, the voice he heard on the road echoed in his mind.

Ananias walked nervously through the streets of Damascus. Could it be true? He had heard a voice telling him to go to Straight Street, where a man named Saul was praying. He was to go to Saul and heal his blindness.

"But I've heard of this man – he's coming to destroy us, just as he's tried to destroy your followers in Jerusalem!" Ananias prayed.

"Just go. I've chosen this man to spread the good news to all – Jew and non-Jew alike."

So Ananias swallowed hard, and walked on to the house. He walked up to Saul and placed his hands on him. "Brother Saul," he said, "I know you met Jesus on the road, and he spoke to you. He spoke to me, too, sending me here so that you could see again, and receive the Holy Spirit."

Then something like scales fell down from Saul's eyes, and he could see again. He ate, and his strength returned. He spent some days with the disciples in Damascus, and then he began to speak in the synagogue, teaching that Jesus was the Son of God. "But this was the man who's been throwing Jesus' followers into prison!" people said. Still, he carried on speaking with astonishing power and wisdom. Many believed at his words, but some were angered by this change in him, and wanted to kill him. So Saul's new friends helped him escape from the city: they lowered him down over the city walls in a basket.

## The Spirit and the centurion

Cornelius the centurion had been watching the galleons sail in and out of the white marble port of Caesarea. Every day these great ships came and went, to and from the rest of the wide Roman empire. He and his family did not follow the Roman gods or Roman ways. They were faithful, prayerful, and generous to the poor. As Cornelius turned away from the bright sunlight, he saw something even more dazzling – a vision of an angel. The vision spoke.

"Your prayers and gifts to the poor have come before God as an offering. Send men to Joppa and tell them to bring back someone called Simon Peter. He is staying at the home of Simon the tanner, who lives by the sea."

Cornelius did just that.

As his men were approaching Joppa, Simon Peter the fisherman was praying on the flat roof. There he had a vision. He saw a huge white sheet let down before him. Inside it were all kinds of animals that the Law of Moses said not to eat.

"You're hungry, so eat!" said a voice.

"No!" Simon Peter replied. "I've never eaten anything unclean in my life!"

This happened three times, and each time the voice answered, "Don't call anything unclean that God calls clean!"

Just then Cornelius's men arrived, asking for Simon Peter, and the voice said, "I've sent men to find you. Just go with them – don't hesitate!" So he went with them.

When Simon Peter went into Cornelius's house, it was the first time he had entered the home of a Gentile, a non-Jew, where "unclean" food was served, and the Law of Moses was not followed.

"Why did you want to see me?" Simon Peter asked, looking around at the crowd of family and friends Cornelius had invited. Then Cornelius told him the vision of the angel.

"So it's true! God really has no favourites," Simon Peter replied. "He wants everyone to follow him!" And he began to tell them about Jesus.

While he was still speaking, the Holy Spirit came, filling Cornelius, his friends, and family with joy, and they spoke in different tongues as the disciples had at Pentecost. Simon Peter and the other Jews who had come with him were stunned that God had given the same gift to the Gentiles. And Simon Peter baptized them. "God accepts them, and so will we!" he said.

# Antioch – "to the ends of the earth"

Jesus' followers went into the Greek lands to the north, and reached the city of Antioch. The good news spread out from the little Jewish community to the Greek people, and many of them became followers of Jesus. Barnabas, a Jewish believer from Cyprus, brought Saul to Antioch, and together they taught Jew and Greek alike. And it was in Antioch that Jesus' followers were first called Christians.

It was also in Antioch that Barnabas and Paul (Saul's Gentile name) were given the task of going out and spreading the kingdom to the whole earth. So Barnabas and Paul travelled north, and east, among the islands and along the straight Roman roads that linked city to city, country to country. In every place they came to, they found a group of Jews and began to teach them. In every place, they were joined by Greeks and others, and many people heard the message and believed. And in every place there were also those who opposed Paul and Barnabas.

Yet wherever they went, seeds of the kingdom were scattered and grew. In Lystra, under the shadow of the mountains, and the temple to Zeus, Paul healed a man who had been lame from birth, as Jesus had done. The people were overawed. "The gods have come down to us!" they cried, and prepared a bull for sacrifice. Paul and Barnabas were horrified and shouted at them to stop.

"We are not gods – we are just men like you! We have come to bring you good news of the true God who blesses your land with rain and crops!" Eventually the people listened. But some Jews heard what had happened, and stoned Paul, leaving him for dead. It did not silence him. When he was strong again, he carried on.

At Philippi, a Roman colony, Paul went out on the sabbath to see if anyone was worshipping. There was a group of women praying by the river, and he joined them, and spoke to them. Lydia, a merchant of fine purple cloth, believed when she heard Paul's words, and was baptized with her household. She welcomed him in to her home.

Paul travelled on to Athens, the heart of the Greek world, then to Corinth, and to Ephesus. The kingdom was growing and spreading, despite the opposition. In Ephesus, Paul's teaching turned the people away from the goddess Artemis, who had a beautiful temple in the city. The silversmiths who made idols of Artemis were furious, as they lost business, and they stirred up the people against Paul.

The angry crowds chased him through the city to the theatre, and the shouting mob roared. For hours, the Greek theatre was a dangerous, murderous place. But, gradually, the city clerk's voice was heard above the crowd as he spoke calmly to the people, and his good sense quietened them.

And in time, Paul's preaching established a growing group of believers in Ephesus.

## Paul writes to the churches

As Paul travelled, he did not forget the small groups of Christians he had left behind: the churches. He prayed for them, and wrote to them. From Ephesus he wrote back to Corinth, helping them learn how they could all work together to be like Jesus' body on earth. Some among them could speak with power: they were like the mouth. Others were like the feet, or the hands: they would serve and help, work and heal. Paul told them that each person was important, as each part of the body is important. And above all, he reminded them to live as one, and to love each other.

*"If I have gifts of tongues and prophecy, if I give to the poor,*
*but have no love, then I am nothing. Love is patient and kind.*
*Love always protects, and trusts, and hopes. Love never gives up."*

His letters were treasured, and read out to all the believers.

Paul's journeys were full of adventure, full of trouble. He wrote again to those he called his beloved brothers and sisters, in Corinth: "I've been in prison, and whipped, and left for dead. I've been beaten with rods, and stones. I've been shipwrecked, spending the long night in open water. Danger has been with me wherever I go."

His return to Jerusalem was hardly peaceful. Many in that city were outraged because Paul taught that it was not necessary to follow the whole Law of Moses, and they accused him of bringing people who were not Jews into the Temple. So, once more, anger and rioting flared up around him, and he was thrown into prison, bound in chains. He was handed over to the Roman commander, whose soldiers stretched him out, ready to receive a whipping. Paul cried out, "I am a Roman citizen. You have no right to whip me without a fair trial!" and the soldiers lowered their whips.

After that, Paul was passed between the Romans and the religious leaders in Jerusalem, yet no charge was brought against him. But it was while he was being kept prisoner by the Romans that he saw the way he must go. God told him of his next journey. "You have spoken of me in Jerusalem; now you will speak of me in Rome!"

So Paul, the prisoner, the Roman citizen, appealed to the emperor, and asked that his case be heard in Rome itself. He was sent by ship through the storms of winter to the heart of the empire. The marble streets echoed to the tramp of soldiers' feet, and music and incense drifted out of the many temples.

There, Paul was permitted to live in a rented house, with a soldier to guard him. He was free to speak to all who came to visit him. He told them about Jesus, and about a kingdom that was very different from the power of Rome. While he was there, he continued to write letters to the groups of believers, the churches, he had left behind. Paul encouraged the communities of believers to help each other, and taught them more of the ways of God. "I keep on asking that God will give you a spirit full of wisdom, so that God will be revealed to you, and you will know him better. I pray that your hearts may see the abundant riches that God has in store for us."

So the churches grew in number and understanding as they shared together. When persecution or suffering affected the believers in one place, those in other towns helped them. For the Roman authorities turned against the churches, and began to imprison and kill those who followed Jesus; and, as the years passed, other emperors unleashed great cruelty against the Christians.

## The vision of John

It was during a time of great persecution that one follower, John, was in exile. He was shut away on the island of Patmos, which shone white in the sunlight and was lapped by the clear blue waters of the sea. And there, while he was praying, he had a vision of what would take place, a vision that would give hope to those who were suffering. This is what he saw.

A dazzling white figure appeared before him, with feet like bronze, and a voice like rushing waters, and a face like the bright shining sun. John fell to the ground, knowing it was a vision of Jesus. "Write to the churches!" began the voice, so he did.

He wrote as the voice like rushing waters flowed over him:

> *"To him who overcomes, I will give a crown of life…*
> *a white stone with a new name…*
> *authority over the nations…*
> *the right to eat from the tree of life."*

Then, John saw visions of heaven, with its dazzling throne. He heard angels without number sing their songs of worship, and he saw those who had died for their faith being given white robes to wear.

Those who had suffered heard this song sung for them:

> *"Never again will they hunger or thirst,*
> *never will they feel the heat of the sun beat down on them.*
> *Jesus will be their shepherd,*
> *and will lead them to living water.*
> *And God will wipe away all their tears."*

John saw that evil would be destroyed in a great, burning fire. All evil's terror, all its nightmare dragons and beasts, would be defeated, and there would be a harvest at the end of all time.

And then, John saw everything made new. There was a new heaven, and a new earth. The bright, clear waters of the river of life flowed from under God's throne, and by its side grew the tree of life. Its leaves were for the healing of all nations, and it bore crop after crop of fruit to eat.

He saw a new city, a New Jerusalem, whose gates were always open. And there was no Temple in the city, for God himself was there; and no sun shone down on it, for God gave it light, and Jesus was like a lamp to light the way. Here, God would live among his people, wiping away their tears. For there would be no more crying and dying and pain. The city shone, full of God's beauty and light, and by this light all the nations of the earth could walk without stumbling.

And John spoke to those who read his words: "Whoever is thirsty can come and drink freely from the waters of life. It is a gift for you.

"And the voice of Jesus says, 'I am the Beginning and the Ending of all things, and I am coming soon!' "